Catching the FinTech Wave

Catching the FinTech Wave

How to Adopt FinTech and Transform
Your Financial Planning Business

Ben Goss

Matador
9 Priory Business Park,
Wistow Road, Kibworth Beauchamp,
Leicestershire. LE8 0RX
Tel: 0116 279 2299
Email: books@troubador.co.uk
Web: www.troubador.co.uk/matador
Twitter: @matadorbooks

ISBN 978 1788039 079

British Library Cataloguing in Publication Data.
A catalogue record for this book is available from the British Library.

Printed and bound in the UK by 4edge limited
Typeset in 10.5pt Aldine401 BT by Troubador Publishing Ltd, Leicester, UK

Matador is an imprint of Troubador Publishing Ltd

Thank you to my wife Jayne and my three boys Christian, Gabriel & Raphael for having endless patience, often on holidays and weekends while I wrote this.

Contents

List of figures

About the author: Ben Goss

As the Internet was taking off, Ben was a strategy consultant for PricewaterhouseCoopers. In 1998, along with two cofounders, he left PWC, qualified as a financial adviser and founded Sort, the UK's first online investment adviser. Today Sort would be called a robo-adviser. Sort took off, delivering regulated advice to over 1,000 people a day before selling to the largest online adviser in the US in 2000, now owned by Morningstar. Ben cofounded Distribution Technology (DT) in 2003 to apply the lessons he'd learned about how FinTech can be used to support high quality investment advice. Today DT's digital service, Dynamic Planner, supports over 7,000 financial advisers, 120 asset managers and many billions of pounds of investment recommendations annually.

Ben studied at Bradford University in the UK and Indiana University in the US where he was a MacArthur Foundation Scholar. He is a Fellow of the Royal Geographical Society and the Royal Society of Arts and is passionate about innovation and the opportunities technology brings to solving important challenges, including the financial advice gap. Ben is an Ernst & Young Entrepreneur of the Year and winner of the Deloitte Fast 50. He has been widely quoted in the press including *The Times, The Financial Times, The Daily Telegraph, FT Adviser, FT Money Management, Citywire* and *Money Marketing* and has blogged for the *Huffington Post*. A much requested speaker, he has spoken at numerous industry events including the UK Government's International FinTech Conference. He writes a regular blog at www.dynamicplanner.com.

Acknowledgements

Much of the original thinking for this book first appeared in my blog at www.dynamicplanner.com. Thank you to all the team at DT, clients, partners and contributors who gave me feedback and helped me refine my ideas.

This book is about best practice in the implementation of FinTech in financial planning, so special thanks go to the many people who have allowed me to share their real-life stories in it as they have sought to grow their businesses using technology. Thanks also to those who gave feedback as the manuscript came together with the shared ambition that a better book would help the industry deliver better outcomes for firms and the customers we all ultimately serve.

Summary

As a busy executive, you might want to skip to the key points without having to read an entire book, so this section provides a summary of each chapter and acts as a directory.

Chapter 1 explains why senior executives in financial advice or planning firms, large and small, should read this book in the first place! In short, it's because applying Financial Technology (FinTech) successfully can help you:

- Massively grow your firm's productivity, reduce your cost to serve and increase your profits
- Transform access to your advice and planning services
- Enhance services so you can retain and grow customers who will be only too happy to pay your fees
- Reduce your compliance risk by building suitability into your firm's DNA

Chapter 2 sets out the five big challenges firms face when seeking to adopt FinTech. These are:

- Solving Rubik's Cube and prioritising what's important in a complex, highly regulated environment
- Getting engagement from customers
- Bringing advisers with you
- Ensuring investment suitability and managing systemic risk
- Building bridges between data islands

Many FinTech projects and programmes founder on the rocks because of these challenges, and often firms don't even start out on the journey because they appear insurmountable. Forewarned is forearmed though; being clear on the challenges is the first step to overcoming them.

Chapter 3 sets out what good financial planning looks like and therefore what the aim of FinTech should be in enabling it. Even though it can take many forms, the essence of good financial planning is *to help customers achieve their goals at a suitable risk and cost*. Critically, good planning encourages the customer to act, rather than plan for planning's sake. There have been many digital white elephants built over the years which offer great technical solutions but are rarely used and even more rarely acted upon.

Chapter 4 explains the importance of investment suitability for customers, firms and the industry and the central role of asset allocation in driving an investment strategy which helps customers achieve their goals at a suitable level of risk. When applying FinTech, asset and risk model (ARM) integrity is key to delivering a consistently suitable investment planning process. It defines ARM integrity as consistency of:

- Risk definitions and boundaries
- Asset class definitions and assumptions

- Language from customer to investment manager
- Data definitions

Incorporate ARM integrity into your technology and it becomes part of your DNA and a powerful engine for your business.

Chapter 5 addresses how you can effectively engage with customers to successfully use FinTech to discuss investment risk when levels of financial capability are often low. It looks at the strengths and weaknesses of the psychometric approach to investor risk profiling and how to address its weaknesses. It also explains how the use of digital in a modern risk-profiling process can help the adviser show even greater levels of empathy and insight.

Chapter 6 focuses on the importance of assessing investor experience and engagement in the risk-profiling process and why assessing the customer's risk capacity is critical. It looks at how FinTech can help you do this well. It also explains how to turn a customer's risk profile into a value-at-risk number which the customer understands and around which you can build a personalised and systematised recommendation they will act on.

Chapter 7 looks at how to build suitability into the DNA of your investment proposition. It examines why there is a large and growing trend towards asset managers managing multi-asset investments against specific risk targets or 'outcomes'. It looks at how risk targeting, done well, can build suitability into the DNA of your investment proposition which is critical as you apply FinTech.

Chapter 8 reviews why technology works well for compliance. It sets out the scientific revolution that has happened in financial planning over the last decade and the enormous compliance benefits FinTech brings in terms of transparency, consistency and audit trail. It also looks at the spectrum of planning services that can be offered from unregulated guidance to regulated advice and the Regulator's support for the greater use of digital in their delivery.

Chapter 9 introduces the following hierarchy of automation and asks "how far can digital go?"

- Level 1: Needs analysis – straight mathematical calculations
- Level 2: Guidance – risk-based assessments
- Level 3: Personal recommendations – risk-based recommendations based on personal circumstances in a specific need area
- Level 4: Holistic planning – personal recommendations across a range of needs

It looks at how artificial intelligence and machine learning are driving intelligent automation in other industries and the potential lessons for financial services. It also sets out the following four barriers to automation in financial planning. Each is behavioural not technical:

- Inertia and the need for conscious, engaged planning
- Lack of trust in a 'black box'
- The amount of data required
- Mental accounting and exponential complexity

Having set out many of the challenges and the background to the use of FinTech in financial planning, Section 2 focuses on the many benefits of adopting FinTech in your business. Chapter 10 demonstrates how FinTech is a powerful enabler of long-term customer relationships and businesses and how these can be built using a consistent long-term asset and risk model.

Chapter 11 looks at the challenges faced by financial planning firms today in serving lower-balance customers or smaller cases. It explains why the hybrid, digital-human model is already proving to be the most successful and sustainable model for addressing this challenge around the world. It looks at the evidence as to why hybrid models—which incorporate some elements of customer self-serve in combination with human adviser interaction—offer an opportunity to profitably engage with smaller cases.

Chapter 12 starts by examining the gulf between Millennials—as digital natives who have grown up with technology—and the traditional industry. It looks at the nature of change that is likely to occur as this demographic enters the world of savings and investments and possible responses to it in a professional practice. It also sets out the implications of not embracing the use of technology in financial planning in what is fast becoming a digital world.

Chapters 13 and 14 provide two key principles and a step-by-step guide to overcoming the five challenges set out in Chapter 2. They are very much 'how to' guides illustrating how successful firms ensure the service they bring to market meets the needs of their target audience in an engaging and compliant way so that customers act. They deal with the most significant initial obstacle firms face and that is prioritising what is important. Successfully adopting FinTech means tackling key issues in the right order and unscrambling the 'Rubik's Cube' of priorities using eight key steps:

1. Identify your target customer groups, their needs and their story

2. Agree your business goals and the scope and channels for the service
3. Get your asset and risk model in place
4. Design the report and outputs
5. Outline the user journey and process
6. Document your planning rules
7. User-interface design
8. Test the service, identify and remove unintended consequences

Chapter 15 asks why engaging customers with financial planning and with digital planning in particular is such a challenge. It underlines the importance of the role you have in designing and delivering a financial planning service as a 'choice architect' and the positive impact this can have on engagement. It examines four strategies used successfully the world over to successfully engage customers with financial planning using digital. These are:

- Golden questions
- Positive financial nudges
- Rules of thumb
- Curated choice

Chapter 16 looks at how intelligent technology is being adopted in other professions and the insights this offers for financial planning and financial advisers. It looks at why advisers are often concerned about the use of FinTech in the planning process and how the most successful businesses engage advisers and keep them on board with FinTech, including:

- Giving advisers a clear answer to the 'what's in it for me?' question
- Showing how the service will make the adviser look good in the customer's eyes
- Providing strong, senior-level sponsorship
- Building a clear vision for a complete process which significantly reduces the time, cost and risk of delivering planning

Chapter 17 explains why the application of rule or model-driven advice creates the potential for systemic risk and how to address this. It provides three rules for managing this risk and how to protect vulnerable customers, as greater degrees of automation are applied. These rules are:

1. Clearly define the scope of your service
2. Understand your asset and risk model and its strengths and limitations
3. Undertake rigorous testing to show that:
   - Customers understand the limitations and boundaries
   - The service undertakes a robust gating to ensure the service is suitable within the boundaries you set
   - Vulnerable customers or customers who are not suitable for the service or who may not understand it are directed to speak to an adviser
   - You actively mitigate any limitations of the tool; for example, checking for contradictory answers and playing back responses for client confirmation

Chapter 18 emphasises the importance of building bridges between data islands. It looks at the often fragmented systems which sit in the back offices of financial planning firms large and small and the challenge these data islands create for firms in terms of automation and ability to scale. It sets out why an integrated, best-of-breed approach to the key systems in your business will deliver greatest benefits in the short and long term rather than looking to buy or build systems which 'cover the waterfront'. It provides a best-practice systems architecture where:

- CRM owns basic details around the customer, their marketing and communications
- Back office owns financials, fees, compliance and workflow (this may be the same as the CRM in an IFA practice)
- A smaller number of platforms or a portfolio-management system master portfolio information
- A specialist risk-profiling and financial planning system supports the planning and advice process
- A customer-facing portal or app aggregates portfolio data including off-platform assets and tracks performance against the financial plan and risk profile. It is the access point for customer-facing tools and automated advice services

Chapter 19 looks further out at how the adoption of FinTech in financial planning will revolutionise the industry over the long term. It picks out the five big trends discussed in earlier chapters that are likely to change the game and what you can do to future proof your firm against them. The five game changers are:

- Simple, automated advice
- Account aggregation
- Social networks

- Artificial intelligence
- Frictionless financial planning

Chapter 20 provides a due diligence checklist for firms considering building or buying FinTech systems while the appendix provides pointers towards 60 independent resources which can help you on your journey, including the latest regulatory guidance on streamlined advice. One of the challenges with writing a book like this is that the industry is evolving rapidly and so some things, for example regulation, will fall out of date over time or become less relevant. Our blog at www.dynamicplanner.com provides regular updates on many of the topics covered in the book.

Introduction

The first waves of a tsunami

The booing finally stopped. I was mortified. I had never spoken in front of 800 people before, let alone told 800 professionals, in this case financial advisers at their annual conference, that their industry was about to change so radically that, like the dinosaurs before them, those who failed to adapt would go the way of the tar pit.

Not surprisingly, experienced, worldly-wise advisers didn't like being told that the future of financial advice was online by a 32-year-old, who a year and half earlier had been a strategy and marketing consultant for a consulting firm. But it was the year 2000, the height of the dot-com boom, and our company, Sort.co.uk, the UK's first regulated online advice business (today it would be called a 'Robo adviser'), had just been bought by mPower, then the largest online advice provider in the US. Eighteen months into our start-up, we were advising more than 1000 people a day online and we felt that anything was possible.

The truth was that neither we nor the company who

had bought us had the slightest inkling of how tough it would be to bring digital to the world of advice in the face of:

- The way that customers actually behave when faced with financial decisions
- Advisers' aversion towards the use of technology in financial planning
- The weight of real and perceived regulatory risk
- The complexities of delivering anything but the simplest of propositions
- The arcane systems infrastructure that has developed in the UK over decades to support commission-driven product sales rather than financial planning

Of course, my audience knew all this intuitively and responded accordingly. Quite reasonably, they didn't spare my blushes.

Seventeen years on and I have learned a lot. In certain respects, I was right in 2000. The future of advice was online, although not in the way that I had expected. More than 80 percent of financial planning is now supported by off-the-shelf, turnkey digital risk profiling, asset allocation and financial planning services. While adoption was not overnight, it followed a tried and trodden path for new technologies as you can see from Figure 1.

Whether you run an independent financial advice firm (IFA), a wealth manager or a bank, there has been a revolution from paper-based, hand-crafted advice to a much more scientific approach to financial planning supported by digital, Internet-based, model-driven systems. But these changes are nothing compared to the tsunami that is about to crash across the industry as the UK finally reaches

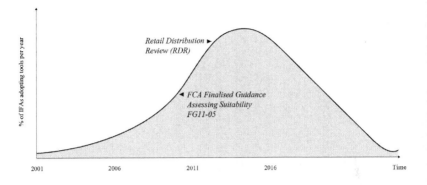

Figure 1: UK IFA adoption of risk-profiling tools
Source: NMG Research IFA Census and DT. Illustrative only

a tipping point where customers, firms, government, the Regulator and systems providers all begin to align to take the industry forward using FinTech.

Why read this book?

"Our firm has grown organically and through acquisition. After the Retail Distribution Review, we successfully segmented our client base and focused on the higher end. Yes, we are profitable but our business is like a swan, we have to paddle incredibly hard under the water to deliver our service. Also for every customer we actively service, we have several more who hold a policy with us but who are uneconomic to support. Can you help?" asked the client. Almost every financial advice and wealth management business in the UK now faces these same questions, and I have been asked them in a multitude of different ways by a multitude of different firms. The challenge is very real: in an increasingly transparent, lower-margin world where there is a far greater focus on risk, how do you deliver a service that your customers need and want, but at a cost, efficiency and risk that is acceptable to you and your organisation?

This book is for senior executives in financial advice firms and financial institutions who are charged with evaluating or implementing financial technology (FinTech)

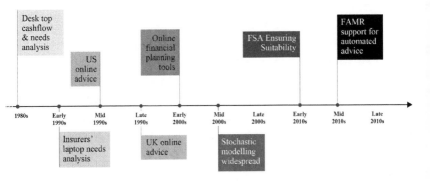

Figure 2: A brief history of FinTech in financial planning

for your financial planning services to help address this challenge. It recognises that the planning process is different from the back office, where technology has been used extensively now for over 20 years.

In the 1980s most back offices relied on paper files and slowly, during the mid-1990s, firms of all sizes implemented technology. This was initially desktop and then Internet-based Software as a Service (SaaS). The planning process, however, was left largely the domain of advisers– constructing financial plans and advice manually on a more or less bespoke basis for each individual customer. With the rise of risk profiling and financial planning systems over the last decade, FinTech has begun to permeate this more customer-facing and therefore more sensitive area. However, its use is still very often limited to specific tasks: building a risk profile and constructing a cashflow plan. As financial planning FinTech develops as a category, the aim of this book is to walk you through best-practice learnings on how to catch the wave as it grows and swells and how to benefit from the vast opportunities it brings, including:

- Massively growing your firm's productivity, reducing your cost to serve and increasing your profits
- Transforming access to your advice and planning services
- Enhancing services so you can retain and grow customers who will be only too happy to pay your fees
- Reducing your compliance risk by building suitability into your firm's DNA

This book takes and shares best-practice learnings from over two decades of experience and will show you how to build a service with FinTech that is strong enough to withstand the five big challenges that all companies face in utilising digital in their financial planning offerings. The learnings apply whether your services are adviser-driven, based around customers self-serving or whether your favoured model is a hybrid of both.

They also apply whether you are a small, local independent financial adviser or a global financial institution. In the digital world, the size of your organisation can be as much a hindrance as it is a help. Yes, the larger your company, the more you can invest in your customer experiences, but the difficulty will be in designing and delivering a truly personal and engaging experience. Larger organisations have multiple teams, multiple systems, more complex product propositions, costly legacy and more heavyweight compliance processes—all of which have to be aligned when delivering a digitally supported financial planning service that engages the customer. This is difficult. Get it right, though, and your brand and channel presence can take a well-designed, well-executed service to millions.

For smaller firms, the challenge is the opposite. How, on limited budgets, can you make the best use of off-the-

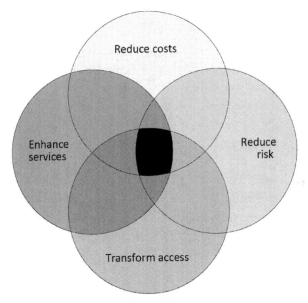

Figure 3: The benefits of FinTech for financial planning

shelf digital services to scale up while making the most of your biggest asset, you? You have built your business based on personal relationships and as Ken Davy, the well-known chairman of SimplyBiz group, once said about his time as an adviser, "The brand that mattered to my clients was mine. I was the one they trusted with their wealth and I was the one they trusted with their biggest financial decisions." The challenge, therefore, when building value in your business beyond you as a key person, is how can you scale your firm and become more profitable using digital but at the same time ensure your clients still benefit from that personal relationship? Get it right and digital can help you get the best of both worlds.

Some shorthand

I frequently use the term 'financial adviser' as shorthand for financial planner, adviser or private client investment manager and the role each may play in building plans, investment strategies or advised recommendations for customers. There are, of course, important differences between each role, but increasingly there are commonalities too.

I mostly use the word 'customer' rather than 'client', accepting that different parts of the industry use different terms; however, it's easier to use a single word. I also use it in part because as digital becomes more prevalent, while some relationships will undoubtedly remain deep ones where the individual or family is serviced regularly over time, others will be more transactional where advice or planning is taken on an as-needed basis—much more like a customer. I use the term 'financial planning' as shorthand for the range of services an adviser might provide: from assessing customer needs or building long-term cashflow plans, to recommending a suitable portfolio or investment. Where it is important to differentiate between these activities, for example for regulatory purposes, I do so. Financial technology, or FinTech as it is known, covers a broad church within a financial planning, financial advice or wealth management business. My focus in this book is on its application to the financial planning process rather than back office tasks or the many other areas in financial services in which technology is now being applied.

The five big challenges in successfully adopting FinTech

This chapter looks at:

- The rapid growth of digital in the UK and how consumer habits and expectations are changing
- The financial planning dilemma; the need for personalisation versus the cost to serve
- The five big challenges in adopting FinTech in the financial planning process

Whether you are a global financial institution looking to deliver a multi-channel digital financial planning experience or a local IFA business passionate about expanding and growing your practice using technology in the planning process, you're facing five big challenges. For those business leaders who are not of the view that change is required, just think about how your customers have evolved even over the last few years. More than three quarters of UK adults now have a smartphone, more than those who own a laptop. Two in five of these people routinely make banking transactions on their smartphone, 11 million people check them within five minutes of waking up and your customers, according to Deloitte's 2015 Mobile Consumer Report[1], check them on average 13 times a day. Yes, 65 to 75 year olds check their device almost every waking hour! Don't even mention the hard-core 18 to 24 year olds who check them 100 times or more a day!

Your customers use technology at work or in their businesses; they bank online; they check and manage their mortgages, loans and credit scores online; they compare and buy expensive holidays and cars with online comparison services; they research and make purchases from books to insurance using apps; and they take advice on almost every aspect of their lives digitally, even their health. On average people are more likely to Google their symptoms if they feel unwell before consulting their partner, family or friends, and only then might they consult a professional GP or pharmacist, according to the 2015 Digital Health Report[2].

The world has changed. The pace of digital adoption means industries are being disrupted at record speed, and that speed is only increasing as mobile spreads and Moore's law continues to make the computer chips in our pockets more powerful—every 18 to 24 months.

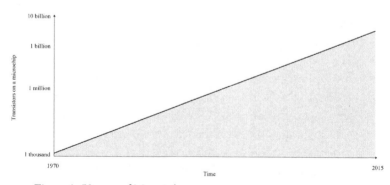

Figure 4: 50 years of Moore's law
Source: Elektormagazine.com, 2015

Is financial planning likely to be immune to this tsunami of digital change? Of course not. One private banking executive described to me how he was in the room with a client and his adviser watching the roll-out of the company's new investment planning service when the 62-year-old client slammed his fist on the desk, making the iPad being used by the adviser literally bounce. "This is unbelievable," the client said. "How on earth have you understood me so well?" He had just had his portfolio digitally analysed and his investment risk profile assessed as part of an annual review. "I've been a client of your firm for more than 20 years and it's always been a fireside chat. This is a massive upgrade. I've been waiting for you guys to introduce some technology." The executive told me later he heaved a huge sigh of relief given he was sponsoring the roll-out. The world is changing even for the most established businesses.

That said, while customer behaviour is evolving rapidly, adopting digital technology is challenging for companies big and small that want to deliver personal financial planning and regulated advice as part of their proposition supported by technology. Some of the largest financial institutions have spent tens of millions of pounds and still failed to successfully deliver digital financial planning with any scale of success.

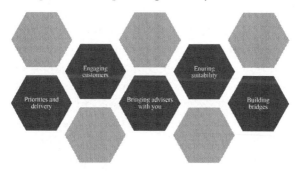

Figure 5: The 5 challenges

So, what are the hurdles they are running into? The answer—based on experience of working with many leading organisations over the last 20 years, from government and the Regulator to some of the top banks, insurance companies, wealth managers and IFAs—comes down to an inability to overcome five big challenges:

1. **Solving Rubik's Cube and prioritising what's important:** Delivering a digital service in a complex, highly regulated environment is difficult. There are lots of competing priorities, each of which should be addressed and preferably in the right order because each has significant implications for the others. Many projects get stuck in this prioritisation quagmire before they even begin, unable to find a successful way through.

2. **Getting engagement from customers:** When it comes to digital financial planning services, profitable, compliant customer engagement is one of the single biggest challenges. Outside of a small number of well-known, well-established brands that appeal strongly to engaged, self-directed investors, there has been very limited success in the UK and internationally in attracting customers digitally without a human adviser involved.

3. **Bringing advisers with you:** It is not only customers who struggle with digital for long-term financial planning; so too do some financial planners, advisers, investment managers, compliance managers and cross-functional teams. Many initiatives that have launched have gone nowhere, stillborn internally because advisers can't see what is in it for them.

4. **Ensuring investment suitability and managing systemic risk:** Introducing inaccuracies into a FinTech-enabled financial planning process could

mean delivering unsuitable outcomes for customers at scale. Avoiding systemic risk has meant that many projects or systems never even leave the drawing board. The compliance function takes a view that it is too difficult and too risky.

5. **Building bridges between data islands:** An industry, where systems infrastructure was built around products and commission plans rather than financial plans, often means that customer-centric data architectures with systems that talk to each other in the right way are just not the norm. The result is often projects whose costs spiral out of control as companies try to build end-to-end systems which 'boil the ocean' or systems which do their job brilliantly but sit in splendid isolation creating islands of data.

This book sets out each of these challenges and provides clear best-practice learnings on how to overcome them. Having misjudged the ease of getting digital financial planning adopted over a decade and half ago, I think it's in all our interests for me to share my findings. Then this time, as the digital wave builds, we as an industry can get it right, so the customers we ultimately serve get access to the quality risk-based financial planning they need, and we get to work in a growing, thriving industry with a strong and exciting future ahead of it.

Section I

What is good financial planning?

Your financial planning business on its best day

This chapter looks at:

- How the essence of good financial planning is helping customers to achieve their goals at a suitable risk and cost
- The different forms that planning can take—from full-blown cashflow plans to simpler multi-asset investment recommendations
- The importance of encouraging the customer to act as the result of a plan, rather than planning for planning's sake

Campbell Edgar, a past president of the Institute of Financial Planning, once told me, "Good financial planning is helping the customer achieve their goals and then ensuring that the cheque to the undertaker bounces!"

While flippant, the essence of good financial planning is implied. You need a plan, and that plan has a long-term objective, which in this case is to 'zero out' the assets on

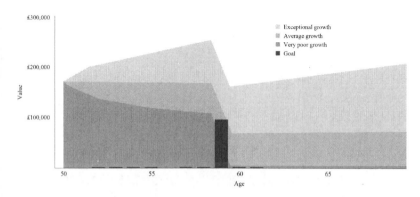

Figure 6: Long - term, risk - based planning

death. It infers that the adviser is there to help articulate and express goals in the first place and then to help the customer along the way if needed. It also implies that the customer takes action. Planning for planning's sake helps no one.

When I look at financial planning businesses across the spectrum, I see that most successful services help customers actually achieve their financial needs and goals over the long-term at a risk and cost that is acceptable to them. A plan might be a full-blown, long-term cash-flow plan with dozens of income and expense lines and 'what-if' scenarios. It might also be a portfolio strategy or as simple as advising on the most suitable investment into which to make regular savings. Each should be suitable for the customer's needs and in particular the risk that they are willing and able to take.

Jim Grant, a very successful entrepreneur and the owner and CEO of independent financial adviser Fidelius, once explained to me that while it may be true that the average holding period of an investment may only be four or five years, the average client relationship in a good financial planning business is measured in decades. You don't achieve this by delivering plans, portfolios or advice that aren't suitable. You achieve customer loyalty through consulting with your customer; helping them explain and test their goals with you; being empathetic; and acting as a coach to help them stay the course over time, particularly when things get tough. *That way the adviser keeps the relationship, even though the investment mix may change.* This is a planning business at the top of its game.

Building plans for planning's sake is not enough. Most financial advisers and financial institutions, on their best day, are about helping their customers make better choices, and implementing and managing those choices, rather than just making plans or selling products, and so that is where the focus of this book is. This is financial planning done well and this is the challenge for digital and FinTech.

The aim of this book is to help you use digital to take your financial planning business on its best day and turbocharge it to be a 'force multiplier'. This is a term the military use when talking about a resource or an attribute that will make a fighting force many times more effective than that same force would be without it.

Best-practice learnings

- Good financial planning helps customers achieve their goals at a suitable cost and risk
- Financial planning is long term. Planning at the top of its game measures relationships in decades
- Planning alone is not enough. The customer needs to act
- FinTech is a 'force multiplier' that enables you and your organisation to achieve a significant multiple of the results possible with a traditional approach

Harnessing a powerful engine: asset and risk modelling.

This chapter looks at:

- The importance of investment suitability for customers, firms and the industry
- The central role of asset allocation in driving an investment strategy to help customers achieve their goals at a suitable level of risk
- Why asset and risk model integrity is key when utilising FinTech in the investment planning process

"Thousands of customers are set for tens of millions in compensation after they were mis-sold risky investments while wanting a safer home for their cash. The company was fined by the Regulator for serious breaches." Google this fictitious new story, which I anonymised from real ones, and you generate a list of household names from every sector of the industry: IFAs, banks, insurers, wealth managers. Whether the problem is caused by a desire to package risky products as safe, a failure of systems and processes or, as it often is, a discontinuity in the way that customers' risk profiles are assessed and investments categorised, the results for the customer and for the company can be disastrous.

"The word we need in the back of our minds, at all times, is suitability. I want it pinned up on the walls of wealth management board rooms; meeting rooms; tea rooms. I want customer service to become institutionalised in this industry," said Martin Wheatley so famously back in 2013 when he was CEO of the Financial Conduct Authority (FCA)[3].

Fast-forward two years to the end of 2015 and the FCA's TR 15/12[4] review of suitability of retail investment portfolios provided by wealth management and private banking firms and a full two thirds of cases fell substantially short of FCA expected suitability standards or needed to make some improvements to meet them. Why? According to the FCA's review often because of, "An absence of up-to-date customer information, inadequate risk profiling, or failure to record customers' financial position and/or their investment knowledge and experience or a risk of unsuitability due to inconsistencies between portfolios and the customer's attitude to risk, investment objectives and/or investment horizon." This is a comprehensive list which shows that ensuring investment suitability is still a major issue for the industry.

At the heart of great financial planning is the ability to help customers trade off risk and return over the long term in a consistent and accurate manner. Most of your customers are not born with sufficient wealth that they can achieve their life goals, including a financially secure retirement. Most need to save and invest for their futures and to take some level of investment risk. Many of those who are born wealthy will need to learn to manage and preserve their wealth with the risk trade-offs this requires. The art of good financial planning is helping customers achieve their goals at a level of risk they are willing and able to take.

The more you use FinTech to support your advice, the more you will need to ensure the accuracy of your asset and risk model. This is your 'engine' and it will power your ship and help you capture the opportunities which flow from the digital wave. It also has a critical role to play in keeping your business off the rocks!

Accurate investor and investment risk profiling is central to ensuring that any financial plan or recommended product is suitable. The risk the customer is willing and able to take, their risk profile, needs to be translated into a strategy that can be implemented. There have been numerous studies on the importance of asset allocation as the principle determinant of the variation of risk and return in a portfolio, most famously one by Brinson, Beebower and Hood originally in 1986[5] and then updated in 1991[6] in which more than 80 percent of the variation in returns was found to be a function of asset allocation rather than

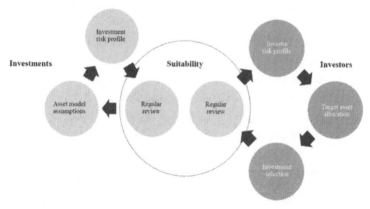

Figure 7: Asset and risk model integrity

timing or stock selection. Translating a customer's risk profile into an asset allocation which delivers that risk and associated range of returns is what successful financial planning businesses do to ensure their customers stand the best chance of meeting their goals at a level of risk that is right for them.

Equal care must be applied when translating the allocation into a portfolio or investment. The investor's mandate to you, as their financial adviser and the asset manager, has to be applied consistently, much as it would if you were an investment manager receiving an investment mandate from pension fund trustees and their investment consultant. The mandate sets out the long-term investment goals, the risk the customer is willing to take and a long-term asset allocation. It may even specify the degree to which the manager can make investments outside of this risk level or asset allocation. It then needs to be monitored on an ongoing basis to ensure the portfolio remains suitable.

To achieve this, a consistent, 'apples for apples' comparison of investor risk with investment risk, it is vital to have asset and risk model integrity, that is consistency across the entire process in your:

- Risk definitions and boundaries
- Asset class definitions and assumptions
- Language from customer to investment manager
- Data definitions

Get this right and you have a strong engine for your firm's financial planning that translates well for digitally supported advice. Get it wrong and you generate problems for you and your customers, with inconsistencies between elements of your process and between advisers.

A great test is whether you can confidently state that if the same customer was profiled by different advisers and offices in your business, would they all reach the same conclusion on a suitable risk profile and investment strategy? The more you use digital in your business, the more asset and risk model integrity will matter.

Best-practice learnings

- High quality asset and risk modelling enables an accurate risk/return trade-off
- Digital doesn't like ambiguity. The more you digitise, the more you will need to clarify and ensure the accuracy of your asset and risk model
- Asset and risk model integrity ensures that investor risk and investment risk are compared on a consistent, like-for-like basis

Financial planning without numbers

This chapter looks at:

- How advisers can engage effectively with customers to successfully discuss investment risk when levels of financial capability are often low
- The strengths and weaknesses of the psychometric approach to investor profiling and how to address the weaknesses
- The importance of digital in a modern risk-profiling process and how it helps the adviser to show greater empathy and insight

A few years ago, in partnership with a leading academic institution, DT commissioned a national polling organisation to ask consumers a series of risk trade-off questions. The technique used was from Nobel Laureate Daniel Kahneman and Amos Tversky's Prospect Theory[7]. The technique involves asking the respondent whether they would take a series of gambles based on the toss of a coin. Each gamble was phrased as follows: "If the coin lands on heads, you win £11. If it lands on tails, you lose and have to pay £10. Would you take the bet?" Variations are then asked: "You win £15 on heads, you lose £10 on tails. You win £20, you lose £10," and so on. Essentially, the theory is that most people are more concerned about losses than gains, which they are, and the aim was to build a predictive model around the theory for UK retail investors. The poll was carried out face-to-face with researchers trained to ask the questions. However, I was stunned by the results. Of the 1,000-plus people tested, the majority answered: "I don't understand the question."

So how do you ensure accurate investor risk profiling and help customers trade off risk and return when most people 'don't do numbers'? We live in a country after all where almost 50 percent of the population can't do basic maths according to National Numeracy[8], a charity dedicated to tackling the issue.

The problem for financial advisers and institutions is that somehow you need to have a discussion (which the customer understands and agrees that they understand) about what the customer stands to lose as well as to gain from an investment, in pounds and pence. If you start a conversation by saying, "How do you feel about a 41 percent chance of losing 32 percent of your investment?" then with most people's level of numeracy you will struggle from the outset.

Many advisers know this intuitively, and some organisations have spent large amounts of money finding it out in practice.

Paul Craven, a former MD of Goldman Sachs and well-known speaker on behavioural finance (his excellent *TEDx* talk on 'Minds and Markets' can be found on his website[9]), makes the point that for financial advisers, it's valuable to know that customers take in information in different ways and learn by using different styles. Some people actually do love numbers, some respond better to anecdotes or pictures, while others prefer to learn by doing and interacting.

The most effective and accurate process used around the world is a multi-stage, multidimensional process, and while it ends with a numeric risk/reward trade-off, it doesn't start there. The start is a robust psychometric questionnaire designed to unearth how someone really feels about the different aspects of investment risk. Investment risk means different things to different people; however, academic studies have shown that a number of factors are excellent predictors of a customer's overall attitude, including:

- Risk sensitivity
- Investment time horizon
- Desire for profit
- Financial awareness
- Tolerance for ambiguity
- Investment experience
- Outlook
- Suggestibility

Psychometrics is the branch of science that seeks to measure personality traits, attitudes and abilities. In essence, a well-designed questionnaire asks multiple questions about how someone feels about each factor and develops a profile that the customer agrees is representative of the way that they feel overall. Much academic work supports the idea that each of us has a certain attitude to risk. In the same way that we tend to be more extroverted than introverted or more agreeable than disagreeable, we tend to feel a particular way about investment risk and this attitude is quite stable over time. A

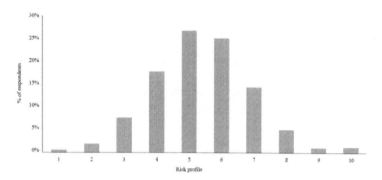

Figure 8: UK attitude to risk
Source: Dynamic Planner, 136,440 respondents, 2015

robust questionnaire should result in a process where you would expect the customer to agree with the profile generated at the end of the process over 90 percent of the time.

While this is a good start, it does mean that out of 100 customers, the calculated attitude to risk could be incorrect for up to ten of them. An airbag that didn't go off ten times in 100 would certainly not get a great safety rating so you need to ensure you augment what should be a great start to your conversation with more discussion and analysis, so that in more volatile markets all your customers are in suitable investments.

It is worth reflecting on the fact that the great strength of psychometrics is that it avoids direct questions to unearth how someone feels. When it comes to regulated advice, however, this can also be its Achilles' heel. Because a customer can answer the same underlying question in different ways, one response can conflict with another. In isolation, a question such as "I would rather put my money in a bank account than invest in shares" answered in a conservative, risk-averse manner states a desire to avoid risk, while remaining questions could be answered in a way that suggest a stronger risk appetite, weighting the final risk profile towards a higher risk level. Taken in isolation, a conservative, risk-averse answer, albeit set amongst other more risk-taking answers, could be the basis of a future customer complaint.

There are several approaches to solving the potential weaknesses in a psychometric approach, including checking the internal consistency of customer responses and ensuring they are aligned. If all questions are answered in a similar manner then a coherent picture builds. If one or more answers are out of kilter then further investigation is required. It could be that the customer has not understood the question, or it may reveal deeper concerns and it's therefore worth exploring. If an adviser is involved, they can use any inconsistencies raised as an opportunity to consult more deeply with the customer and really drill down into their concerns and views. This is one of the great benefits of using an interactive, digital process with customers, rather than a paper-based one. The discussion can be had in real time and helps the adviser deliver and demonstrate insight into the customer's situation.

When automating more extensively it's critical to ensure inconsistencies or questions which may not have been understood in a psychometric instrument are flagged to the user and opportunities are given to clarify in an interactive manner. The FCA in their Finalised Guidance FG1105[10] highlighted the risk of a customer completing a questionnaire and frequently selecting a middle answer such as 'I neither agree nor disagree' as a sign that the client actually may not understand the questions being asked—or may not be engaging sufficiently with the questionnaire. Done well, an automated flag or challenge demonstrates to the user that your service has a level of intelligence and is truly personalising any advice. As a result, it is more likely that the customer will buy into any advice you provide and take action down the line.

Another benefit of digital is the data that can be generated from the risk-profiling exercise. At DT, its independent financial planning advisory board looks at the aggregate output of tens of thousands questionnaires each quarter to find ways to enhance their accuracy. This is an evolving field and there is no substitute for continual refinement based on evidence and big data sets.

Finally, the risk profile description itself is vital. Essentially, this is what will be turned into the 'investment mandate', and so you need to make sure it is in plain English and understandable by the customer. The FCA says it should be 'fair, clear and not misleading'.

Some people prefer pictures, and so using a graphical scale can be helpful, as can showing people where they sit on a spectrum versus others in the population. Framing where someone sits on a spectrum of other investors, from risk avoiders to active risk takers, is very powerful. Many studies have shown that broadly there is a normal distribution of risk attitude in the investing population from strong avoiders to strong takers, with the bulk of the population sitting somewhere in between.

Best-practice learnings

- Most people find it difficult to understand numbers. You need to find a way to talk to them about investment risk without confusing them
- Psychometrics are a proven means of measuring

personality traits and how someone feels about taking investment risk and a good starting point

- Psychometric responses taken out of context can be dangerous and these pitfalls need to be managed. This is particularly true when automating an advice process
- The risk profile description itself is vital and needs to be in plain English and 'fair, clear and not misleading'

Investor experience, risk capacity and value at risk

This chapter looks at:

- The importance of assessing investor experience and engagement in the risk-profiling process
- Why assessing the customer's risk capacity is critical to the profiling process and how FinTech can help you do this well
- How assessing the risk the customer is already taking can provide a valuable baseline for discussion
- How to systematically turn the risk profile into a value-at-risk number which the customer understands and around which you can build a suitable recommendation

Engagement and experience

As an adviser, the level of engagement your customers have with their finances will vary. However, most are not avid DIY, self-directed investors; if they were, they would be doing it themselves. Your customers are by their nature advice-seekers, people who are looking for a trusted source of personal advice to help them understand their choices and which ones are likely to be best for them given their circumstances and goals.

Understanding a customer's level of engagement and experience is therefore an important part of the risk profiling and investment planning process. Talking at DT's annual conference in 2015, the then FCA Investment Specialist, Rory Percival, commented that the level of rigour demonstrated when assessing investor experience was often behind the individual's attitude and capacity for risk.

On the other hand, in its publication *What makes an investor experienced?*[11] the Financial Ombudsman Service (FOS) gives an overview of several case studies where the individual's level of experience has been used as a key rationale for an adviser's recommendation. Reading some of the FOS rulings, it's clear that a client's experience of holding a particular product is insufficient justification on its own for making a recommendation. It is the client's engagement with that product and understanding of it combined with their attitude and capacity for risk which should drive the assessment of suitability. Just because someone has a defined contribution pension scheme acquired through their employer, for example, does not mean to say they are comfortable with or understand its risk.

The FCA provides guidelines in the Conduct of Business Sourcebook[12] on what particular aspects of experience are relevant to consider when making a recommendation. These include:

- The types of service, transaction and designated investment with which the client is familiar
- The nature, volume, frequency of the client's transactions in designated investments and the period over which these have been carried out
- The level of education, profession or relevant former profession of the client.

Today most firms include a discussion around experience as part of the fact find and most good psychometric questionnaires include experience and engagement as factors to be assessed. FCA commentary suggests, however, that many advisers rely on conversations with clients without always documenting these in an effective, auditable way.

When applying more digital automation to assessing experience and engagement, it's worth considering building a more explicit assessment into your risk-profiling process. Where the customer has significant engagement and experience, this can be used as a factor in favour of supporting a riskier investment assuming their attitude and capacity also support this. If a customer has little or no experience of investing or does not naturally engage with the investments they do hold, then it's doubly important to ensure they understand the nature of any risks associated with recommendations.

Investment risk the customer is already taking

If the customer holds existing investments then a very powerful step is to show them the risk they are taking today based on the same spectrum as their risk attitude. This entails gathering information on their current portfolio, plotting it on the risk spectrum based on the weighted average of their asset class exposure and then running these classes through a covariance matrix (a matrix which shows how the performance of each asset class is related to each other asset class) to ensure correlations are accounted for. It is not possible to complete this step efficiently without FinTech as it requires accurate valuation points and the x-ray of current holdings to assess their underlying asset allocations.

If a customer is currently only invested in cash then that provides a good comparison point for any alternative future strategy. If they have been investing widely over many years or decades then it is quite likely that they will have a diverse range of arrangements and risk positions. Examining these separately and in combination is a worthwhile exercise in itself, providing an opportunity to discuss portfolio efficiency and the value that a more structured risk-based investment process can bring.

Risk capacity

Once a customer's attitude to risk has been assessed, understanding their capacity to take risk on is key. While a customer a few years away from retiring might be very comfortable with taking risk, for example, if doing so could significantly impair their standard of living and ability to achieve their goals then good financial planning points out their more limited capacity and builds a plan around this. Conversely, a 22-year-old investing in a workplace pension for the first time has decades before they can access their investment and as such potentially has a much greater capacity to take on stock market volatility during their journey.

Risk capacity can also vary by goal or objective. The payment of university tuition fees for the next year versus the desire to retire, stop working and start living off accumulated wealth in 20 years have very different time horizons and therefore can have different investment strategies attached to them, even if the customer's attitude to risk is the same.

Risk capacity should assess:

- Investor timescales
- The customer's ability to withstand financial losses on their lifestyle or not achieve their goals
- The customer's potential need for liquidity / to gain access to to their investments

A powerful way to check capacity is to stress-test current and prospective portfolios and show what would happen in an extreme bear market, the impact on goals and the likelihood of needing to access the capital. You can bring this to life by illustrating what would have happened in historic market downturns; for example, October 1987's Black Monday, 1992 and Britain's exit from the European Exchange Rate Mechanism, 1997 and the Asian financial crisis, 2000 and the dot com crash and 2008's global financial crisis. With a digital financial planning service comes the ability to show the customer interactively how their portfolio and any prospective portfolio would have performed under extreme conditions based on the underlying asset classes and look at the impact on their overall assets, income, goals and lifestyle.

Value at risk

Once you have accurately assessed the customer's attitude to and capacity for risk, you can have a meaningful discussion around 'value at risk'. This is the first time numbers will be involved and requires the adviser to set out options from low to high risk. The most intuitive approach for this conversation is to create a series of equally spaced model asset allocations each with progressively greater potential risk and return, so that the adviser or the digital service can allow the customer to look at the trade-offs. Using cash as the anchor and emerging market equities as the most volatile asset class makes a lot of sense for the majority of retail customers.

For example, at one end of the spectrum if a customer invested £100 in cash over one year, they might gain back an additional £1 (after inflation), but then they might lose £3 because of inflation. At the other end of the scale, if the customer invested their £100 in emerging markets, great performance might deliver a 30 percent return (£130), but poor performance could lose them as much (£70). With an intuitive digital graphic, the adviser and customer can explore the range of potential risks and returns, looking at numbers in the short, medium and long-term and in particular looking in depth at risk profiles one or two points above and below the customer's attitude score. Customers and advisers alike find this discussion highly engaging and it helps gain buy-in to an agreed strategy.

The short-term value-at-risk figure needs to be accurate and derived from history and from looking at the distribution of potential future returns, which may not have shown up in history yet or recently. Done well, it prepares the customer for the bad times, which will surely

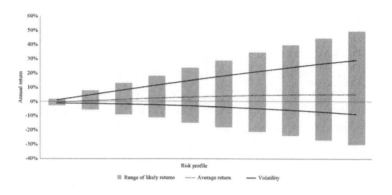

Figure 9: Value at risk
Source: Dynamic Planner, illustrative

come in any long-term investment, so you're able to say, "Remember, we talked about this. Let's stick to the plan."

Financial institutions do this exercise regularly, some daily, and use varying degrees of likelihood; for example looking at what would happen to their balance sheet in a catastrophic event or series of events that might only occur one year in 100 (i.e. one percent of the time). The fifth percentile (i.e. five percent of the time or a 'one in 20- year storm') is a good balance between helping retail customers understand the level of potential losses they might face in their portfolio but not scaring them rigid with the losses associated with an even rarer event. Good financial planning is helping customers prepare for the future and act with knowledge of the risks, not frightening them into inaction!

While risk is important, return is why customers are investing. It's important to strike the right balance. Telling the performance story within the context of the risk the customer is willing and able to take is key.

With this understanding, the customer can select a profile that reflects how they feel, their experience and engagement levels, their capacity for risk and where they feel comfortable with a value at risk. Ideally, they can do this in the knowledge of where their current savings and investments sit on the same scale.

Once the profile has been agreed, the question then is: how do you ensure that any investment recommended meets this profile? The answer comes down to consistent investment risk profiling, and this is discussed in the next chapter.

Best-practice learnings

- Understanding investor experience is important, however, don't rely on it as a proxy for engagement, attitude or risk profile
- Risk capacity is not the same as a willingness to take it. Consider the customer's time horizon, liquidity needs, and ability to withstand losses or not meet goals
- Selecting a suitable investment risk profile means selecting a profile that reflects how the customer feels, their experience, their capacity for risk and where they are comfortable with the value at risk

Building suitability into your DNA

This chapter looks at:

- Why there is a large and growing trend towards asset managers managing multi-asset investments against specific risk targets or 'outcomes'
- How the institutional pension fund and private client investment management worlds have approached risk management in a similar way
- How risk targeting done well can build suitability into the DNA of your investment proposition

At one of DT's annual off-sites, Gary Potter came and spoke to DT's team. Gary and Rob Burdett co-head the BMO F&C Multi-Manager solutions business, and their Lifestyle Funds comprised one of the first risk-targeted fund ranges when it was launched back in 2007. The funds have been run to follow the Dynamic Planner asset allocations for risk profiles three to seven since inception. Today, they manage more than £880 million of customers' money, deliberately targeting the allocations and risk level for each profile while making their own investment selection decisions.

Many of the team—developers, testers, client success associates—never get to meet a fund manager, so they peppered Gary with questions: "Why do you follow these allocations?", "How do you do it?" "What happens if you have a different view?" Gary explained: "For advisers, the Lifestyle Funds provide consistent propositions that can easily be aligned with defined client types; and assuming no change in client attitude to risk, they remain suitable at the outset and for the duration of an investment. This alignment is obviously beneficial for the client too, as the asset mix they hold is one that is suitable for their needs—a peace-of-mind investment that shouldn't throw up any nasty surprises." Gary explained that the team don't just follow the long-term model, however. Within each fund, they can tilt away from the target allocations for each sub-asset class by +/– five percent, while still remaining within risk profiles. This enables them to tactically move the portfolios towards investment styles more suited, in their view, to benefit from prevailing market conditions

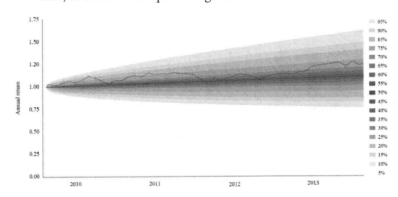

Figure 10: Risk targeting
Source: Dynamic Planner, risk profile target asset allocation performance

Using risk-targeted solutions is a great way to build suitability into the DNA of your investment process within your firm. They are built and managed to deliver to your customer's risk/return mandate, helping them achieve their goals at a risk they are willing and able to take. Combined with a digital app or portal which tracks the customer's portfolio and risk against the agreed risk profile, there is a great opportunity to demonstrate value to a customer so they are happy to pay your fees!

In the institutional pension fund management world, money management has worked using risk targeting for decades. An investment consultant talks to the pension fund trustees about their current assets and potential future liabilities and agrees an asset allocation that the scheme is comfortable with. It will be one which should deliver the level of growth and income to meet those potential liabilities at an acceptable risk. The consultant then translates this strategy into one or more investment mandates to be executed by selected investment managers, with or without the ability to stray outside certain limits to drive performance or manage risk. The consultant ensures a consistent definition of risk boundaries, asset class definitions and the same asset class expectations in terms of returns, volatilities and correlations, translating these from the pension fund's requirements to the individual managers.

In the retail world, almost all external asset managers you use will have a different set of risk and asset class definitions, a different vocabulary, a different set of assumptions and a different investment philosophy. This makes sense insofar as there are lots of different ways of managing money and many different philosophies. The challenge for advisers is mapping these different approaches back to the risk profile and definitions agreed with the customer. Do it consistently, and you achieve asset and risk model (ARM) integrity—end-to-end consistency from the customer to the asset manager and suitability in the DNA of your investment planning. Do it badly, and you create a systemic disconnect which can lead to customer detriment.

Many private client investment managers (PCIMs) have sought to use a form of risk targeting, running discretionary portfolios against the objectives and mandates agreed with the client. It is the institutional model scaled down for the individual or family. The challenge for many PCIMs, however, is that it's extremely difficult to maintain and document suitability for many hundreds—or, in the case of larger firms, thousands—of portfolios in line with client needs. Doing so manually is costly and you run the risk that the portfolio becomes unsuitable if not actively and regularly rebalanced.

Given the level of oversight needed for each portfolio, wealth managers are increasingly utilising model portfolios for all but their highest-net-worth clients. They are also introducing more structured guidelines and FinTech allowing managers to know their client, assess their risk profile and objectives, and then monitor and rebalance their portfolio. Many discretionary investment managers also now provide models which IFAs can access for their clients. Some of these are available as unitised funds. IFAs benefit from the outsourcing of the investment-management process within a risk-profiling and investment process they trust.

As risk profiling has gained greater traction, more and more asset and portfolio managers have adopted the concept of risk targeting, explicitly stating that their funds or portfolios are designed to stay within a particular risk profile. This makes the adviser's job easier and lower cost, and helps ensure ongoing suitability while ensuring no nasty surprises for the client. The most effective approach to risk targeting relies on a strong risk-profiling process upfront which sets expectations for what the normal range of gains and losses might be and what might happen under more extreme circumstances. The aim is to ensure that the investment is managed such that 95 percent of the time losses are never greater than the value at risk discussed with the customer.

Risk targeting should be a dynamic, forward-looking, proactive strategy based on asset allocation and the investment process, rather than solely relying on a rear-view mirror assessment of historic volatility. It does not seek to provide guarantees against losses, and customers who require these should be taking lower levels of risk, if any investment risk at all.

Assuming risk targeting is achieved successfully, it is more likely to mean that the tenure of individual funds and managers increases as they deliver against the customer mandate, rather than being 'fired' for performance or not delivering against the latest performance story or fashion. As such it's a positive development for all.

Best-practice learnings

- Aligning the investment risk profile with the customer's risk profile on an 'apples for apples' basis helps ensure asset and risk model integrity and embeds suitability into the DNA of your proposition
- Monitoring investments against a specific definition of risk is critical to ongoing suitability. Done well, it's not

just an assessment of historic volatility but a review of current asset allocation and investment processes

- Risk targeting is gaining greater traction as more investment managers manage their funds or portfolios to stay within a particular risk profile. This makes the adviser's job easier, lower cost, lower risk and helps ensure ongoing suitability

Why FinTech is great for compliance

This chapter looks at:

- The scientific revolution that has happened in financial planning over the last decade
- The compliance benefits of FinTech in the planning process in terms of transparency, consistency and audit trail
- The spectrum of planning services that can be offered from unregulated guidance to regulated advice and the Regulator's support for the greater use of FinTech in their delivery

A scientific revolution

"As I'm talking, I'm just looking at your eyes, and when I mention the word 'risk', for instance, I can tell what sort of risk you want to take... trust me, I've been doing this a long time." You only need to watch BBC *Panorama*'s 2011 documentary 'Can You Trust Your Bank?'[13] to cringe at examples of the 'bad old days' of investments sold without a structured assessment of risk or suitability. Going back even further to 2004, when NMG consulting[14] first started tracking how risk assessment was completed, this was the norm, with 80 percent of advisers determining a client's attitude to risk through a 'general discussion'. I remember sitting with the director of a national advice firm back then; he looked at me for a moment and said, "Ben, I just don't get it. When I sit with my clients I have this" – he lifted a pen – "and this" – he pointed to the back of an envelope – "and it works just fine."

Over the last decade there has been a scientific revolution in the way in which financial advice firms undertake risk profiling and investment planning. Much of this has been catalysed by the Regulator, particularly the FCA's Finalised Guidance on Assessing Suitability in 2011. It has also been driven by a realisation by firms and institutions that the conversation with the customer is too variable, too inconsistent and too important to form the basis of an investment plan without the accuracy and audit trail that specialist systems bring.

When it comes to regulated advice, FinTech can help

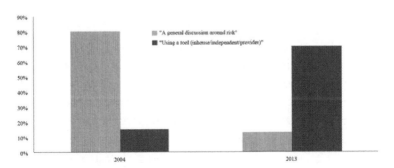

Figure 11: A scientific revolution
Source: NMG Consulting, IFA Census

financial advisers provide a level of transparency and record-keeping which is a world away from the 'conversation on the couch'. Using technology requires financial planning rules to be coded into 'ones and zeros' and your organisation to take a clear view on its asset and risk model and compliance rules. The result with a good system is therefore not only an auditable record of the inputs associated with each customer and each piece of advice but also of the model and rules used. These can be stored and referred to if required should the customer ever come back to you with a concern or a complaint. This data can also be analysed to see emerging patterns, for example, the distribution of customer risk profiles in your business, by adviser or by region, or the differences between customers' attitudes to risk and final risk profiles selected. Aggregated analysis gives your business an insight into how customers are being advised as well as trends over time which will help with your regulatory reporting, governance and oversight.

The use of FinTech in this way is increasingly being encouraged by the Treasury and FCA. In their 2016/17 business plan[15], the FCA put access to advice —specifically, "Affordable, accessible advice options that meet consumers' needs"—right at the top of the list of the outcomes they are looking for. Ensuring that "Advice, including low cost advice, is delivered in innovative and accessible ways" is third on their list of five. Tracey McDermott, acting FCA CEO at the time, gave a speech on the regulation of advice post the Financial Advice Market Review (FAMR)[16] that further underlines the FCA's ambition to make it easier for firms to adopt FinTech across the spectrum of delivery mechanisms: "Take, for example, 'robo-advice' (which we prefer calling automated advice by the way). While it won't be for everyone, it has the potential to be an extremely effective way of providing more affordable and engaging advice for many consumers. For those who prefer face-to-face advice, we are also seeing several hybrid models which give people the option of speaking to an adviser at some point during the automated process. And it's not just about automated advice—technology can also play a role in traditional advice. For example, development of portable fact finds and shortening overly lengthy suitability reports which FAMR recommends could lead to real progress in reducing the cost of traditional face-to-face advice." Without doubt, at the time of writing the FCA and the Treasury now see FinTech as the way forward and have significant ambition for it within the industry.

In 1998, when we went for regulatory approval for Sort under the then regulator, the Personal Investment Authority (PIA), we had a relatively simple time interpreting most of the relevant rules in the Handbook. Where anything was unclear, we agreed an approach with the appointed liaison officer, and then applied this to the letter with all customers—many thousands of them; at one point, more than 1,000 a day. We passed our supervisory visit that year with a clean bill of health, and it became clear to us, our compliance officer and our PIA supervisor that the transparency and auditability of digitally coded services were very powerful from a compliance perspective.

While the Handbook still exists, since 2007 the industry has operated under principles-based regulation. Today, it's outcomes that matter, not just the process. In particular, Treating Customers Fairly requires firms to operate not only through systematic box-ticking but also by ensuring that the customer understands the advice they have been given and that the scope of any service is appropriate for their circumstances. The advice itself, of course, should be suitable and communicated in a manner that is fair, clear and not misleading. In Chapter 17 I look at what successful firms are doing to ensure that their FinTech services meet this challenge, including working with the FCA's Project Innovate and particularly with its Advice Unit[17] set up as a result of FAMR to assist firms in adopting automated advice processes compliantly.

The spectrum of services

It is worth noting in this chapter the evolution of non-regulated advice, which FAMR also sees as offering potential for firms and customers alike. On the spectrum of financial planning—from needs analysis and goal planning, asset allocation strategy and product-type guidance, through to investment-specific advice—only investment-specific advice is a regulated activity. As organisations have begun to look at customer self-serve solutions, many have considered whether they want to cross the line from providing unregulated guidance into regulated advice. To date, relatively few have chosen to provide guidance because of the concern that it may be viewed as advice by the Regulator and the Financial Ombudsman Service (FOS) if a customer was to make a complaint.

As a result, in 2015, the FCA sought to clarify the boundaries in its Finalised Guidance 'FG15/1: Retail investment advice: Clarifying the boundaries and exploring the barriers to market development'[18]. It provided a framework, explaining when an activity might be guidance or regulated advice, regulated advice being when advice is given to a potential investor on the merits of buying, selling or holding a specific, regulated investment product.

There remain grey areas, however, with many firms feeling that guidance can still be caught as advice because it pertains to a regulated product even though a personal recommendation as to the product being suitable for that customer's circumstances has not been made.

The final report from the FAMR published jointly by the Treasury and the Regulator[19] in March 2016 recommended that this be addressed and that: "HMT should consult on amending the definition of regulated advice in the existing Regulated Activities Order (RAO) so that regulated advice is based upon a personal recommendation, in line with the EU definition set out in the Markets in Financial Instruments Directive (MiFID). This has now happened and the Government will change the law from January 2018[20] to bring the definition into line with MiFID for regulated firms.

In summary, investment advice will involve the provision of a *personal recommendation* to a customer, either on their request or at the firm's initiative. It will comprise three main elements:

- There must be a recommendation that is made to a person in their capacity as an investor or potential investor
- The recommendation must be presented as suitable for the person to whom it is made or based on the investor's circumstances
- The recommendation must relate to the person buying, selling or otherwise transacting the investment

Almost certainly this will mean more firms see the provision of information and digital guidance as an attractive low cost option, including on the risk profile of available funds and generic strategies, such as topping up an ISA. However, because these services will not be able to present something as suitable to the customer, it remains to be seen how effective they will be at encouraging customers who are not already self-directed to act. This is particularly so because personal recommendations will not have to be explicit, they could be implied. For example, a firm might provide an implicit personal recommendation, according to HMT; "if it is presented to the customer in a way that would influence the customer to choose a specific financial product over others, for example by making a statement such as 'people like you buy this product'."

Best-practice learnings

- There has been a scientific revolution in the assessment of investor risk over the last decade bringing far greater accuracy, consistency and compliance
- FinTech can help you ensure suitability, transparency and record-keeping which is a world away from the 'conversation on the couch'
- The FCA and the Treasury now see FinTech and the greater use of automation as the way forward for the industry and through Project Innovate have provided a range of resources available to firms wishing to adopt technology and automation

The hierarchy of automation: how far can digital go?

This chapter looks at:

- How use of artificial intelligence and machine learning is driving intelligent automation in other industries
- The hierarchy of automation in financial planning from simple needs analysis to more complex, holistic planning
- The four barriers to automation in financial planning

"This mystery author and her archaeologist hubby dug in hopes of finding the lost Syrian city of Arkesh." "Who is Agatha Christie?"

Watching IBM's Watson super computer beat champion human players in the US quiz show *Jeopardy!* is fascinating[21]. Watson's speed, its cognitive powers and its ability to get answers right before the human champions had even understood what was being asked, is deeply impressive. Not only did Watson have to work out the answers to questions, but it actually had to figure out what the questions meant in the first place using natural language. On the day of the test, Watson had access to 200 million pages of structured and unstructured content consuming four terabytes of disk storage, including the full text of Wikipedia. In training, Watson IBM engineers played more than 100 games against past winners in order to improve its chance of winning, significantly developing its artificial intelligence since its predecessor, Deep Blue, beat grandmaster Garry Kasparov at chess.

Watson is a highly-evolved example of the application of massive computing power and machine learning where computers can learn without having every single step explicitly programmed for them. For other, more day-to-day examples, think about how Google finds information for you, how Amazon suggests products you might want to buy, or how LinkedIn figures out whom your connections might be. These algorithms have learnt how to do this through data, rather than being pre-programmed. That's also how Google's driverless cars have over a million miles

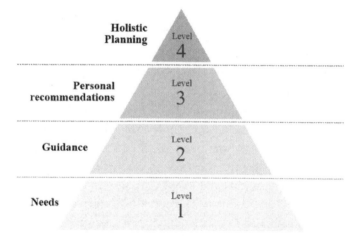

Figure 12: Hierarchy of automation

under their belt without causing accidents; they have learned how to tell the difference between a human and a tree, and what to do about it. As FinTech is increasingly applied to financial planning, a key question to ask is how far can automation take us?

Financial planning activities can be categorised into a hierarchy, from those that can be more simply automated to those that are more complex:

Level 1: Needs analysis—straight mathematical calculations
- What financial needs and goals do I have? For example, will my dependents be financially secure if I die? How much do I need to save to have a financially secure retirement?
- What might my cash-flow and savings look like in the future if I saved more or lost my job?

Level 2: Guidance—risk-based assessments
- Which needs should I prioritise?
- How much risk am I currently taking with my investments?
- What is my attitude to risk and ability to take it?
- What's a suitable asset-allocation strategy?

Level 3: Personal recommendations—risk-based recommendations based on personal circumstances in a specific need area
- Which specific investments in which combination will stand the best chance of achieving my strategy at a suitable cost and risk?
- Which products should I invest in or sell, in which order, to maximise the benefit of tax and product features?

Level 4: Holistic planning—personal recommendations across a range of needs

- What cash-flow strategies and financial arrangements should I put in place to help achieve my goals and maximise the benefit of tax and product features across multiple needs?

Is it feasible that a customer's financial plan could be built that gathers all the necessary data and constructs a path from Level 1 to Level 4 through a lifetime accumulation of assets, and then a suitable glide path through decumulation? The answer must be 'yes'. Assuming the data is available the algorithms required are certainly no more complex than those required to automate in other industries. How likely is it that the automated advice from a machine would be acted upon by either an adviser or customer? The answer would have to be 'unlikely'. Why? There are four barriers which need to be addressed for automation really to take hold.

1. Inertia and the need for conscious, engaged planning

Most people are not engaged with their long-term finances and find the whole area difficult. I will explore this more in Chapter 15; however, when it comes to automation it means involving customers in their financial decisions; gaining the data needed to automate and then encouraging them to act is a challenge from the outset. Further, financial planning requires the customer to make conscious, risk based decisions about their future, for example, agreeing to draw down their pension and take an investment risk and postpone taking an annuity for a few years in the hope that their health worsens and they get a better rate. These are frequently emotionally charged, risk-based choices in which customers need to be active participants, not passive passengers. Overcoming inertia is a challenge from the start.

2. Lack of trust in a 'black box'

Early on in DT's history we built a black box, a 'financial ecosystem' which effectively optimised the right level of investment for a customer to achieve multiple goals across multiple financial needs: investing, retirement, protection, mortgages and cash-flow management. The ecosystem had all sorts of assumptions built into it about risk levels, inflation, life-styling (i.e. moving into less risky assets as the customer approached each goal), recourse rules (i.e. which products should be accessed first to pay for goals) and rebalancing, alongside financial planning rules such as the amount customers should hold in an emergency fund or the proportion of expenses that would be required annually by a customer if their spouse were to die. This was all technically correct, but it generated huge numbers of questions about what was going on in the black box, and, counterintuitively, meant that advisers and their customers took *less action*, not more. Taken together with inertia and the lack of trust in financial services more generally (see Chapter 15), automation on its own is unlikely to deliver the financial planning action needed.

3. The amount of data required

The amount of data to be gathered from the customer to automate at the top end of the hierarchy would be enormous; not just hard facts about the customer's current arrangements (financial and non-financial) but also soft facts about how they feel, their goals and ambitions, and their aspirations for the future. Even with the empathy and consulting skills of a good financial adviser, it is hard to keep someone sufficiently engaged to elicit all this information, let alone ensure its accuracy. To build algorithms which delivered complete automation, not only would extensive customer data be required from the individual being advised but to ensure suitable outcomes huge data sets would be needed from a wider population to test the algorithms and see what worked for others like them. These data sets are beginning to be built; however, they are not there yet.

Of course, the moment the digital ink is dry on the plan, life happens; and customers' lives change. They lose their job, or get divorced, they get a promotion, or their partner gets sick, they get an inheritance, or their home gets flooded. The plan is then out of date, and either irrelevant or in need of a whole new calibration and the process starts again.

4. Mental accounting and exponential complexity

Mental accounting is the phenomenon first named by Richard Thaler[22] whereby people treat money differently and mentally place it in different 'pots', depending on factors such as the money's origin and intended use. Organisations the world over have run into issues when trying to replicate or codify this phenomenon into planning services. One response to this is to enable customers to set up multiple accounts, each of which is assigned to fund one or more goals. Each goal might have a different time horizon and risk level attached. A portfolio then has to be built to meet each goal and suitable product wrappers found for each portfolio or possibly elements thereof. The result in some implementations is that the complexity of user experience grows exponentially as portfolios are nested in products, which are nested in goals.

Advisers use very human shortcuts or heuristics to cut through this issue rather than figuring out the optimal mathematics as the mathematics can often generate unintuitive solutions which customers feel are complex or unsuitable. While it is technically possible to overcome this phenomenon, given enough time and money, to date it remains a barrier to full automation.

These experiences frame my view that while there is no technical reason why financial planning cannot be fully automated, the behavioural barriers are significant. The most successful approach to digital is to make financial planning choices as easy and engaging to understand as possible, breaking up a larger plan into smaller, simpler questions and decisions, and helping customers understand the trade-offs that each implies. This task-based approach does not insist on a holistic assessment.

If you look to other industries, you see the same thing too. Technology is great at taking individual tasks, automating them, and adding intelligence and insight to them. Think about hailing a taxi through Uber, buying a Chinese dinner through Just Eat, or booking a hotel through Booking.com. None of these services try to push you through a holistic assessment of your needs, a prioritisation of which option is right for you and then a recommendation and purchase. No, they address a single piece of the value chain and make it easy and engaging for the customer to decide and then act.

Best-practice learnings

- There is a hierarchy of automation from simple needs assessment to holistic planning. The higher up the hierarchy the more challenging automation becomes
- It is not technology that limits automation, rather there are important behavioural barriers
- The most effective automated propositions address specific tasks lower down the hierarchy, rather than holistic planning, and break them into simpler, easy and engaging tasks

Section 2:

Catching the wave: using FinTech as a force multiplier

Building your business on strong foundations

This chapter looks at:

- How long-term customer relationships and businesses can be built on a consistent long-term asset and risk model
- The importance of investment risk profiling and risk targeting to ensure suitability on an ongoing basis
- The range of investment strategies emerging from asset managers to provide risk target managed solutions

Speaking at a DT conference, Malcolm Streatfield, CEO of Lighthouse Group PLC started his talk with a story; "Late at night in rough seas a US Navy aircraft carrier signalled to another vessel that it should change course. The carrier received back a response that they should be the one to change. The captain of the US carrier repeated his demand, identifying himself and the ship: 'I am the captain of a US Navy aircraft carrier. You must change your course.' The response came back: 'I am a lighthouse. It's your choice.'"

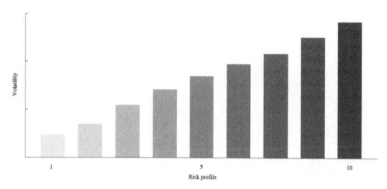

Figure 13: Risk profile coherence
Source: Dynamic Planner, ten-year annualised volatility by risk profile to 2015

Like the lighthouse, what shouldn't change in any long-term financial plan is the risk mandate the investor has set, unless of course their goals or circumstances change. I understand now what Malcolm was saying: without a need to respond to the latest investment news or short-term investment story, the great strength of a financial plan based on a long-term asset and risk model is its consistency. It is the foundation on which long-term customer relationships, and indeed businesses, can be built.

During the global financial crisis in 2008, I remember many meetings with financial advisers who told me that having a long-term, risk-based plan in place made conversations with customers far easier at a difficult time. Their customers were being bombarded with unsettling news about the stock market and, not surprisingly, it made them nervous. The advisers were able to address customer concerns, taking them back to the plan and the risk-based discussions they had had, and say, "Remember, we talked about this. These events can and do happen. Stick to the plan." I recall one adviser simply saying that his clients rarely called. He had always discussed value at risk with them during the planning process and so they were well prepared.

While no one can reliably predict the future or the timing of very rare and extreme events, it is possible to describe the range of returns investors might experience most of the time as well as in more extreme circumstances. An accurately calibrated model, particularly one delivered digitally in an engaging manner and used interactively with a customer to help them see 'what if', means that during a market downturn the nature of falls come as less of a surprise. While few people are happy to lose money, the customer understands the bigger picture and has had their expectations set. As a result, they are more comfortable riding out rough seas.

Accurate investor risk profiling is only half the picture. The other half is ensuring that the customer's investments are profiled accurately to ensure suitability not only at the point of advice but also so that they remain suitable. Done regularly and well, investment risk profiling provides a vital part of the chain a firm needs to ensure suitability on an ongoing basis. If the investment drifts and begins to change its asset allocation or other risk characteristics, customers can be informed and advised accordingly. With a discretionary mandate the manager can rebalance and bring the portfolio back into line with the agreed risk profile.

As discussed in Chapter 7, there has been a significant growth in advice firms with centralised investment propositions who are now actively targeting investor risk profiles using a range of investment strategies. These strategies include: low-cost, passive solutions which seek to deliver the risk benchmark with minimum cost, active fund management who follow the risk target but seek outperformance through tactical tilting and manager and security selection, and discretionary portfolio managers who run models or private client portfolios to achieve the same thing.

As the need to deliver ongoing suitability at lower cost grows across the industry, so this area will grow, much in the way that multi-asset funds have grown from marginal to mainstream over the last decade.

Best-practice learnings

- The great strength of a financial plan based on a long-term asset and risk model is its consistency. It is the 'rock' on which long-term customer relationships and businesses can be built
- An accurately calibrated model, particularly when used digitally and interactively, helps manage customer expectations and understand value at risk
- Investment risk-profiling services ensure an ongoing, objective analysis of an investment's make-up and management

Accessing the customers that traditional services can't

This chapter looks at:

- The challenges faced by financial advice firms today in serving lower-balance customers or smaller cases
- The ageing customer base of many financial advice businesses and the problem this represents
- The emergence of the hybrid digital-human model as a successful and sustainable model

I was presenting at an adviser roadshow in the West Country and joined a group of three seasoned practice principals for lunch afterwards. They said, "We have a problem and we'd like to know if you can help… We're worried that our clients could die before we have a chance to reach the next generation." Like many successful firms, they had migrated their business model away from commission to fees post-RDR and had a profitable practice. They had focused on 55 to 75 year olds, 'pre-', 'at' and 'in' retirement, and most of their clients had £100,000-£300,00 invested with them, some considerably more. They grew through referrals, and where they could, they politely declined customers who didn't fit their desired profile. They used a risk-profiling service to deliver a consistent investment and suitability process with a well thought through, centralised investment proposition to manage suitability risk. In most respects, business life was good.

Except, their valued customers kept referring their sons and daughters, nephews and nieces and friends who didn't meet their segmentation criteria. Even the valued clients themselves, when it came to ISA season or when they had 'a little bit of money to invest', would frequently need advice on smaller amounts. The practice principles said: "We have built these relationships over a long time and we are trusted. The problem is, it's a lot of work to advise on an ISA for £15,000. We do it because we don't want to disappoint our established client, but we lose money every time. Can you help?"

As the conversation progressed, another, more strategic, challenge emerged. They recognised that their customer base was ageing and that one day the partners would want to sell the practice, so it was important it maintained good long-term prospects. "We're worried that our clients could die before we have a chance to reach the next generation. We need to find a way to engage with them digitally."

Looking at the data below you can see that this is not a firm-specific issue, but an industry phenomenon. Of the more than 180,000 cases that were planned in Dynamic Planner in 2015, the largest proportion of customers were aged 55 to 59 for men and 60 to 64 for women; 73 percent of males and 74 percent of females were aged 50 years or over. They are Baby Boomers.

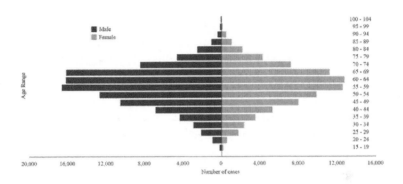

Figure 14: Clients are getting older
Source: Dynamic Planner, clients planned, 2015

We talked for an hour about what the scope of an ideal service might be for this demographic, how much they thought their customers would be willing to do digitally and how any business would ideally be transacted post-advice. They had given it a lot of thought.

In essence, their view was that their clients, young and old, had to play a much more active role for the advice process to be profitable, particularly for smaller cases. The firm wanted to retain the personal relationship, brand and investment proposition for which they were trusted; however, they also wanted the customer to be able to engage with a streamlined self-service, digital process which followed the same principles of the risk-profiling and suitability process they used face-to-face. It would be a hybrid; not fully fledged digital automation but not solely reliant on manual methods either.

This hybrid model is gaining traction in the US. Fidelity[23] published research in 2016 which showed that what they call eAdvisors (i.e. practices that have embraced digital technology) have 40 percent more assets under management than traditional advisers. Aite (well-respected analysts in the wealth-management space) also published a study[24] in collaboration with BNY Mellon and Pershing showing that advice firms adopting digital technology were growing faster than those that weren't. They listed several capabilities used by digitally enabled advisers and these included: using a tablet when meeting with clients, working remotely with clients, offering client access to statements on a client portal, providing client access to real-time portfolio information (holdings, balances, activity) and providing adviser-client collaboration tools (e.g. chat, co-browsing) via web or mobile.

Another report published by Cerulli Associates, a respected analyst in the US market[25], predicted a convergence between robo-only and human advisers as opposed to the dominance of one particular model. The report stated: "Both types of providers are moving toward a model that combines online advice with human support." Cerulli see this convergence being driven not just by a desire to acquire Millennial customers (i.e. customers born between the mid-1990s and early 2000s), but by the fact that Generation Xers and Baby Boomers can be just as attracted to digital offerings and, indeed, increasingly expect digital as part of the process. More than 30 percent of customers for Wealthfront, the US market leader in pure robo advice provision, for example, are over 50, according to the report. A range of other in-depth studies, including from Heidrick & Struggles with the Centre for Financial Planning in the US[26] which summarises the potential future into four technology-enabled scenarios, and Roubini Thoughtlab's study[27] of 2,000 investors and 500 investment providers across ten major wealth markets map out similar hybrid dynamics.

From a West Country IFA practice to US analysts and institutions, the same pattern is emerging: the answer for financial advisers and institutions is a hybrid of digitally supported advice through FinTech in combination with human beings. This hybrid model uses digital to get customers to do more, so that your cost to serve falls while you keep your business and the trust that your customers have for it and you at the centre of the relationship.

Best-practice learnings

- Post-RDR segmentation means that while firms may be concentrating on higher-value, profitable clients, lower-balance clients and smaller cases are still part of the business mix and are costly to serve
- An ageing customer base poses challenges for firms looking to build their businesses for the future or retain value in their business for an exit
- Hybrid models which incorporate some elements of customer self-serve in combination with adviser interaction offer an opportunity to access lower-balance customers profitably

Dumped by the wave: manual businesses in a digital world

This chapter looks at:

- The gulf between Millennials as digital natives who have grown up with technology and the traditional industry and the radical change this will bring
- The nature of change and possible responses to it in a professional practice
- The implications of not embracing the use of technology in financial planning

A few years ago, I was asked to speak to a lecture room full of students at Oxford's Saïd Business School. I explained what I did and how we supported financial advisers in their provision of financial advice. When I finished, I got no reaction at all; the students just sat there in silence. Finally, one raised his hand and asked: "Why do you give this technology to advisers? Why don't you just give it directly to us?"

    This is the gulf between generations. The Millennials, now in their teens to early 30s, expect to do much more digitally and through help and advice from their social networks, they are digital natives. Baby Boomers approaching or in retirement, on the other hand, expect to use an adviser because this is how the industry has grown up with them over their lifetime. As Millennials get older and wealthier, their financial lives will also get more complex and the need for professional advice will no doubt grow. However, their starting point is so vastly different, it can't help but have a dramatic impact on your business as they begin to earn and inherit wealth.

For those of you heaving a sigh of relief at the thought of radical digital change being at least a few years off, think again. Richard Susskind, a well-known lawyer and author who studies the impact of technology on his profession, divides the legal world's short-term evolution into three stages:

- Denial: Where lawyers deny that they really need to change the way they work
- Delivering legal work differently: This is all about cost and risk reduction through automating existing processes and specialisation within the practice
- Disruption: "The tasks involved under the heading of lawyer will change. A lawyer in 2025 might be a legal process analyst, a legal project manager, a legal knowledge engineer. Over the next decade, I don't see there will be a reduction in the number of lawyers, but there will be a great change in the nature of what they do."[28]

Post-denial, technology can do two things: it can help an industry do what it is already, but faster, cheaper, better, or it can help it do things differently (Susskind's disruption).

As set out already, the financial planning industry post-RDR is already having to do things faster, cheaper and better, and with lower risk. Pre-RDR profitability was a function of what level of commission was gained from product providers, rather than how efficient an operating model was. Once commission was removed, underlying operating models were exposed and most firms have found that the demands of true profit and loss and cash-flow management in a fee-based world require the adoption of FinTech now—not in a year's time, but now.

In 2011, the FCA provided guidance on suitability which, while aimed at process, focused on the practical use and calibration of risk-profiling systems, providing examples of good and bad practice. Subsequently, other consultations have provided further clarifications for firms using technology both to drive down cost and risk in their business (Susskind's second step) and to look at delivering access to financial advice differently (the third step). As described in Chapter 8 the FCA is strongly encouraging this.

Looking at another industry, in 2004 the Association of British Travel Agents published research[29] showing that agents were more trusted than the Internet, with 75 percent of package holidaymakers saying they used agents as a source of information. Less than ten years later, by 2012

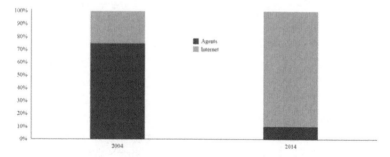

Figure 15: Trust in travel agents
Source: ABTA 2004, Mintel 2012

this position had been completely reversed, with figures from Mintel[30] showing that 70 percent of people who took a holiday in the previous year booked entirely online, and fewer than 10 percent now believed that travel agents were better informed about holiday destinations than professional bloggers or review websites such as TripAdvisor.

While financial planning is not the same as holiday planning, similar forces are at work including:

- The widespread adoption of broadband and mobile technology
- Customers' comfort with researching and purchasing goods and services online
- Product simplification and transparency

Many senior executives in financial advice firms and financial institutions will comfort themselves with the fact that change will take some time, and that as buying an investment is not the same as buying a holiday, the traditional role of the adviser will remain for some time yet. While this is true, it is important to note how quickly change happens once the ball begins to roll. As Bill Gates so famously said, "We always overestimate the change that will occur in the next two years and underestimate the change that will occur in the next ten. Don't let yourself be lulled into inaction." Financial advice firms and financial institutions need to prepare now or risk being dumped by the digital wave.

This happens because of 'tipping points' resulting from the alignment of demand with the availability of a complete product that other people you trust are buying, not just the early adopter 'geeks' who love playing with new things. Just think about how strange the Toyota Prius was when it arrived in 2000. Only a die-hard early adopter who liked to be different would be seen dead in one. How strange would it be to buy a hybrid now? Not very. They are sensible mainstream choices. The same will be true in financial services around customers gaining advice from or purchasing from FinTech-powered services.

In the direct-to-consumer space over the last few years, innovators have launched services hoping to resonate with the mass market but appealing thus far only to a small number of early adopters. Over time this will change, not least because others will learn from the mistakes of those innovators and get their proposition more right than wrong. You only have to look at the advice gap and the 5.5 million customers Deloitte believe[31] are going unserved to see a significant market opportunity in this space.

Best-practice learnings

- Over the next ten years Millennials will earn and inherit more. They have been trained to access advice digitally and through their social network in other areas of their lives, they will expect digital as part of any service you provide
- Cost and risk reduction through automating existing processes and specialisation within the practice are key and this is a well-trodden path
- Running a manual business in a digital age is increasingly unprofitable and risky with the Regulator publishing guidance on investment advice process which can only successfully be implemented using FinTech

Section 3: A step-by-step guide to overcoming the five challenges

Two principles

This chapter looks at:

- The multifaceted nature of the challenges organisations face when developing a FinTech financial planning service
- The two key principles you need to adhere to for successfully designing and implementing a new service

In this chapter and the next I'll set out the key principles and a step-by-step guide needed to successfully design and implement a new FinTech planning service in your organisation, whether it is adviser-driven or customer self-serve or a hybrid. These principles and guide are based on my experience over the last two decades working with a wide range of clients—including the Treasury, the Regulator, banks, wealth managers, insurance companies, investment platforms and financial planning businesses large and small— to apply FinTech to the financial planning process.

In 2004 DT worked with the Financial Services

Authority (FSA) on a consumer detriment analysis for Basic Advice[32]. When the FSA was considering a change in regulation, they usually did this by asking a panel of experienced advisers to comment on fictitious customer cases, showing how the change would impact outcomes. In this case, they also used our rules engine configured to FSA advice requirements to augment their assessment and provide a 'benchmark' for advice for 503 customer cases. They then compared the manual outcomes to the digital ones and set out the findings in consultation paper 11/04.

In Annex D of the consultation paper there is a lot of discussion around why good advice can vary and the wide range of considerations that need to be taken into account to ensure a good outcome for the customer. This is not surprising in an industry that is used to delivering advice manually. Codification takes a great deal of thought, and deciding what practice you will adopt in your firm or institution will require the same.

The more automated the service, the more complex the planning rules are. The hierarchy of needs and prioritisation algorithms, tax, investment and drawdown rules (which products to save into or access first when taking money out), life-styling and rebalancing approaches, emergency fund strategies, annuity rates, goal funding... the list goes on, and all this is in addition to the core asset and risk modelling methodology. While software models can cope with the breadth of this multivariate analysis, each of these facets and their relationship with each other needs to be coded. So, the problem becomes very big, very quickly, and many digital financial planning projects struggle.

In my experience, though, it's not only the rules which cause problems, it is building a planning service which:

- Incorporates an accurate asset and risk model
- Is engaging and reflects behavioural finance principles to encourage customer action
- Ensures suitability, is compliant and treats customers fairly with oversight and audit trails to prove this
- Is scalable, secure and performant
- Is integrated from front to back office to ensure relevant customer data is available and processes can be completed on a straight through basis
- Meets your business objectives and reflects product marketing and sales priorities

Many projects and cross-functional teams get stuck trying to align all the sides of this Rubik's Cube before they even begin! To address this challenge, successful programmes almost always follow two key principles:

Principle 1: Stay lean

Financial planning is such a broad topic that it's easy to expand the scope of your project or proposition and try to meet too many needs at once. Until your financial planning service is being used in anger, you won't know what's important to customers, what they will buy or use and therefore what to expand further or stop.

The Lean Startup[33] approach to product development provides a great framework for delivering a Minimum Viable Product to users initially; i.e. deliver a service/app which meets the minimum needs of the user sufficient for them to buy or act with before evolving it further *based on real feedback*. Once you get that feedback, you can either persevere with your plans, and continue to build out the service in the direction you started or 'pivot' and change direction, responding to the feedback. Lean Startup encourages regular reviews to pivot or persevere to minimise the time spent pursuing features or functions that users don't value and maximise the chances of success.

For example, over the first two years post-launch of Dynamic Planner's risk-profiling app, there were three major evolutions, but in between there were a dozen or more monthly releases in which the service was tweaked or extended based on feedback from advisers; each time the app was tweaked in the right direction, adoption grew faster. Some tweaks were very small, while others much larger, but each was based on regularly gathered feedback from advisers and based on their experience with customers. Today it's the most widely used app of its type.

Principle 2: Assign a trusted financial planning 'architect'

Cross-functional teams often struggle with digital financial planning projects because they require such diversity of inputs across a business. Over the years, I have seen projects fare best when they have a 'financial planning architect' as a central part of the team. The architect is a trusted, experienced subject-matter expert who has the delegated authority to make functional design decisions in the context of the business's objectives. The architect needs to understand both business goals and customer outcomes required as well as the vision for the service. He or she needs to be comfortable working with colleagues who have strong user interface and user experience design skills, as well as those from IT, compliance and other functional areas. The really good architects are often senior financial advisers or come from a planning background. Without this, they struggle with the domain experience.

Best-practice learnings

- Stay lean. Financial planning is such a broad topic, it's easy to over-expand scope of a new proposition, and until people are using the new service in anger, you won't know what you need to evolve
- Appoint a 'financial planning architect' as part of the team. This trusted, experienced subject-matter expert will help provide the glue to your project team in an area where domain expertise and experience planning with customers is critical

Eight steps

This chapter looks at:

- The importance of establishing a clear target audience for your service early on with clear business objectives for the service
- The eight steps needed to develop or configure a successful FinTech financial planning service
- How successful firms ensure the service they bring to market meets the needs of their target audience in an engaging and compliant way

Building or implementing engaging, compliant and effective FinTech-supported financial planning processes is challenging for the reasons set out in the previous chapter. That said, to catch the digital wave organisations need to do it and do it well. This chapter looks at best practice and how successful firms deliver their services, whether these are built to order or more commonly configured from a white label service.

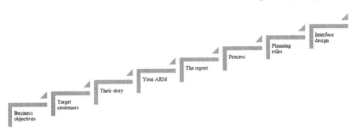

Figure 16: 8 steps to success

Step 1: Identify your target customer groups; what are their needs and what's their story?

You need to clearly agree your target customer groups upfront and summarise these into two or three personas. A 'persona' is a clearly identified example customer with particular needs and situation. For example, you might build a service for customers in their 40s with moderate savings who want to start seriously investing for their future or a customer in their 50s who wants to ensure income security in retirement.

For each persona, it is very helpful to build one or more user stories. A story might start: "Steve Smith is 45 and he and his wife are thinking investing his bonus of £30,000. His father is a client of your firm and Steve has contacted you for some advice." Once you know whom you want to target and what service you are looking to provide, you should clearly test whether such a service makes sense to the customer. Successful services use one-on-one research, discussion groups and quantitative and qualitative questionnaires to help identify and refine their service propositions. Asking experienced frontline advisers will also generate significant, expert insight.

Step 2: Agree your business goals and the scope and channels for the service

With your target audience in mind the next step is to agree the business goals for your service; for example:

- To service lower-balance customers or smaller cases economically
- To attract new customers who are likely to become the profitable customers of the future
- To retain and develop existing customers who are not actively serviced
- To provide a portfolio review service so customers really see the value of your advice and are happy to stay and pay your fees

While this might seem simple, many propositions are not clear on their goals or take on too many competing objectives. This is a guaranteed formula for doing few things well and drowning under the weight. In any business, there are competing initiatives and so being clear on priorities is critical.

With any service, there is a decision to be taken regarding the channels you will use to deliver it. Adviser only, digital only or a hybrid of both. Increasingly successful firms are taking a hybrid approach often extending the planning technology they are using in their business to deliver elements of their service digitally.

Step 3: Get your asset and risk model in place

As discussed in previous chapters, the asset and risk model will act as the engine for your service and drive both the outputs and the inputs you need. While it might seem counterintuitive to a customer-led user design, the reality of many projects is that without taking this step first and getting a sound model in place, you run the risk of defining a user experience which either can't be delivered with a robust methodology or designing a process which doesn't capture the right data in the right order to deliver suitable outcomes.

With the asset and risk model in place, you can then look at the range of analysis you want to present to the customer. For example, one approach might be to tell a customer how much they need to save to achieve an agreed level of income in retirement. Another might be to tell them how much income their current level of savings will give them, or to signal whether they are likely or unlikely to meet their financial goals. There are lots of variations on the key financial planning questions and a good model will be able to provide accurate answers for the range of outputs you want to provide. It also may be that you have existing data on your customer, like their portfolio value, portfolio constituents or their asset allocation, and you want to factor those in. Again, a good model will be able to help you look at the different outputs and insights you can achieve and the inputs you will need to achieve them.

One of the benefits of using an off-the-shelf planning service is that a good vendor will have thought about these issues and created processes which capture the right data in the right order to support suitable outcomes for the questions.

Step 4: Design the report

Before you build the process, you need to think about the

output you want to provide to the customer and the actions you want them to take. A financial plan or suitability report is a very tangible way of doing this onscreen or as a downloadable report. An investment recommendation report, for example, might include:

- Actions to be taken
- Needs or objectives to be met
- Risk profile (attitude, experience, capacity, value at risk)
- Summary investment strategy
- Specific investment recommendations
- Reasons why recommendations are suitable, referencing needs and objectives and strategy
- Possible disadvantages or risks of pursuing this course of action
- Costs and charges in cash and percentages
- Signposts to product disclosures and risk warnings
- A playback of the customer's situation (fact find)

It's easy to get carried away with technical analysis, graphics and intricacies of the user journey and forget the essence of the plan you are trying to create. The key question to ask is: does the plan tell a clear and compelling story that the customer will understand and is likely to act upon? Mocking up a plan's report to test with customers, advisers and compliance is an excellent means of testing a digital proposition. With positive feedback you are in an excellent position to develop or configure the rest of your service. A further consideration is whether the plan provides a good basis for an ongoing service and relationship, for example, with the ability to track portfolio value and risk, target asset allocations and progress against goals.

The Association of Professional Financial Advisers

(APFA) provide excellent guidance on suitability reports including a ten-point checklist in their guidance publication, *Smarter Communications and Suitability Reports*[34]. It was developed after discussions involving APFA, the Personal Finance Society, the FCA and the Financial Ombudsman Service.

Step 5: Outline the user journey and process

Once you are clear on who your users are, their situations, the problems they are trying to solve and the action you want them to take, you are then able to sketch out your desired journeys and share them with prospective users to see whether they have the right effect. At this stage you're trying to understand whether the broad shape of your solution meets the user's expectations and needs. The detailed design of the analytics, content, graphics, graphs and charts can come next. At each stage, you're able to change the journey based on feedback from users and it's a lot easier and cheaper to change pencil drawings than code. The key at this stage is to construct an overall process which:

- Is engaging to the user (see next chapter on the techniques successful firms use to achieve this)
- Collects the financial planning inputs needed
- Can generate the outputs needed for the plan

The initial wire framing is best completed through a series of workshops in which designers and the financial planning architect can describe the process flow they are looking for. Experts who understand the asset and risk model, financial planning rules and technical architecture can input into it too. Once available, the process should then be tested again to check that it is likely to generate the user responses you are seeking. A by-product of this process is that the wire-frames can quickly be turned into a non-functional prototype to be used as a powerful illustration or internal sales tool.

Step 6: Document your planning rules

In parallel with Step 5, financial planning rules and calculations need to be documented. The benefit of using an established model is it should have tried and tested calculations available for review. This speeds up the process, saving significant time and money and the risk of getting these wrong with consequences downstream. Check with your wireframes to ensure you can collect all the inputs you need to achieve the outputs. You may need to loop around these two steps a few times to ensure it all works as expected.

Step 7: User-interface design

Financial graphs and charts get complicated for even the most sophisticated financial advisers and customers, so the last thing you want is additional complexity from the user interface. With smartphones now leading the way in which the Internet is accessed, supporting mobile needs to be a key design principle. For user-interface design, it is worth having workshop sessions with your financial planning architect, user-interface/experience designers, asset model experts and developers, to look at how planning information can be displayed to get the desired analysis across as effectively as possible while minimising inputs. Presenting the results to end customers on a regular basis is fundamental to success, to ensure they are taking what you had hoped for from the process. Testing and refining your approach enables you to understand what matters to your users—including the things you've not thought about.

Step 8: Test the service, identify and remove unintended consequences

It is important to know that your target audience will react to the service in the expected way. It is also important to identify where people for whom the service is not intended aren't unwittingly using it and receiving unsuitable planning or advice. You should be particularly careful around 'boundary cases', ensuring that those for whom the service is not absolutely suitable are managed properly. Testing is a question for careful consideration and one I address in more detail in Chapter 14.

Best-practice learnings

- Identify your target customers early on and what they need from a financial planning service
- Ensure you are clear on the business objectives of the service to avoid scope creep and a service that tries to meet lots of needs without absolutely delivering on one
- Before you work on the user journey, think about the output you want to provide to the customer and the actions you want them to take

How to engage customers

This chapter looks at:

- Why engaging customers with financial planning is such a challenge
- The importance of the role you have in designing and delivering a financial planning service as a 'choice architect'
- Four strategies used successfully the world over to engage customers with financial planning using digital

When it comes to digital financial planning services, profitable, compliant customer engagement is one of the single biggest challenges. Outside of a small number of well-known, well-established brands that appeal strongly to engaged, self-directed investors, there has been very limited success in the UK and internationally in attracting customers digitally without a human adviser involved. This represents a significant challenge not only for financial advisers and institutions but to the country overall. Post-RDR it is now accepted that an advice gap has been created in which consumers who are not engaged enough with their finances to make sufficient long-term provision for their retirement are unable to access the professional advice they need, because the cost and risk of advice delivery has been too high. Digital channels with their low marginal cost therefore represent a potential game changer as a means of creating innovative access and this is a top priority for Government and Regulator alike.

So why, almost 20 years after my cofounders and I started Sort.co.uk, the country's first regulated online advice business, has digital made such little impact in the landscape? Why hasn't it been embraced by consumers and what is standing between them and the advice they want and need?

There are three principle reasons for this lack of engagement.

Reason 1: System 2 thinking

The first is that financial planning is not like planning a holiday or buying a car; it requires slow, thoughtful, 'System 2' thinking, according to Daniel Kahneman in his book *Thinking Fast and Slow*[35]. Many initiatives have gone nowhere because customers who are 'not engaged' struggle

Figure 17: 3 reasons customer engagement is challenging

to envisage a future and the trade-offs needed today in order to delay gratification. Even US studies[36] of mature online advice services show that when offered online financial advice as part of their pension plan very few customers (five percent) use it. It's very difficult to point to the benefit in terms of improved savings levels or outcomes.

Reason 2: Financial capability

Secondly, multiple studies[37] have shown that levels of financial capability, defined by the FCA as people's ability and motivation to act in addressing their financial situation, are extremely low in the UK. Why?

- Risk aversion: Decisions often entail risk taking and committing to the unknown. Most people are inherently loss averse (see Chapter 5) and place more value (often twice as much) on avoiding losses than achieving gains. Many people seek to avoid regretting choices and feel that doing nothing is better than making a choice you live to regret.
- The complexity of investment products: Investments are intangible and abstract with lots of strange features and charging mechanisms. According to PWC[38] many people have concerns over poor performance and overcharging.
- The length and speed of the learning cycle and the feedback loop: Test-drive a car and within minutes you are learning about the nature of your choice. Buy a pension and it may be years before you know whether it was a good choice—with considerably more financial commitment! Understanding the nature of the risks

you face and what might be suitable for you is much more difficult when the feedback loop is so long.

• Trust: While some areas fare better than others, financial services is the least-trusted[39] consumer sector. A large part of this may be the result of failures in certain parts of the market, but lack of trust remains a huge barrier for financial services practitioners to overcome. Misselling episodes, where unsuitable products were sold to customers who didn't understand or didn't have the capacity to take on the risk, weigh heavily in the public consciousness.

Reason 3: The tyranny of choice

Thirdly there is the issue of choice. In a famous experiment[40] conducted by Sheena Iyengar of Columbia University and Mark Lepper of Stanford, in an upscale California grocery store, researchers set up a sampling table with a display of jams. On the first Saturday, they offered an array of 24 different jams to taste, on the next Saturday they displayed only six. More shoppers stopped at the display when there werev 24 jams, but when it came to buying jam, 30 percent of those who stopped at the six-jam table went on to purchase, as opposed to only three percent of those who were faced with the selection of 24. Too much choice can be demotivating.

Other studies have found similar results in US 401(k) pension plans. These plans offer huge incentives to participate, including tax breaks and employer contributions. At the same time, typically they present a huge amount of choice. The researchers observed: with just two choices, 75 percent participated, but with 69 choices, only 60 percent participated. With more than 2,000 investment funds available for sale in the UK, investment selection is not for the faint-hearted.

Faced with these challenges it is no wonder consumers often struggle to engage with financial planning and to make decisions and act without professional advice from a trusted person.

Your role as a choice architect

So, what can be done to engage customers? The first step is to recognise the role that you play when you provide a financial planning service. In designing or configuring a digital financial planning service, Cass Sunstein and Richard Thaler would call you a 'choice architect'[41]. A choice architect is someone who designs the way in which choices are presented to users and who is conscious of the impact of this presentation on decision-making. You do this in a traditional face-to-face business of course, with good financial advisers engaging and selling to customers by asking questions which encourage them to make positive choices. Some advisers will be better at this than others and the very best will often modify their approach based on individual customers. With digital, however, even if it is only a component of your service proposition, the choice architecture is codified and therefore your process will be pre-prescribed, even if it is a dynamic process, so it needs a lot of thought beforehand.

Sunstein and Thaler recognise that you can 'nudge' a user into making better decisions not only through the choices offered but also through *how* they are presented. The key to this is understanding that it's better to make active, informed design choices where the implications for the user and their experience have been explored than to simply focus on the business or functional needs of a process. Behavioural finance and the role of nudges are on the Treasury and Regulator's agenda too. The FAMR report (see page 49 onwards) reflects Government thinking that nudges and rules of thumb are important in encouraging customers to engage with their finances and as shortcuts to comprehending what good financial planning looks like. Again, good financial advisers often do this anyway using heuristics or shortcuts to help their customers understand their situation and the implications of certain choices.

Before engagement can really begin, however, it is important to establish the right context for a customer. Because of the long-term, system 2 nature of financial planning, for most people it only moves 'front of mind' as the result of thinking about a life event or a financial event. These might include the birth of a child, marriage, a new job, redundancy, buying a home, education, retirement, getting a bonus or inheritance or concern about death or illness.

At this point, the first port of call for many will be family and friends or online. Where it is online, it might be a Google search for informational or comparison websites, or if you have an existing relationship with the customer it may be your website. For younger customers it's more likely to be social media and networks[42]. The best services provide relevant and engaging online content which helps to *educate* the customer on their situation, potential needs and some of the *non-product-specific strategies* they can take to help meet them. Given that at this point in their journey most consumers have limited financial capability, investing in this content is key.

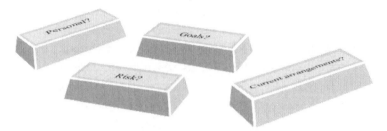

Figure 18: Golden questions

This is not a marketing book, and there are plenty of texts and resources on how to develop and market successfully using content relevant to your audience. Whether you are running a small advice practice or a major financial institution though, relevant content to an audience in need of an objective education is a necessary first step to engaging with financial planning.

Technique 1: Golden questions

Having generated a level of interest through your content and education, the process of engaging around the customers' personal circumstances can begin. The first technique used by successful digital services is asking 'golden' questions. These short questions get customers thinking about their personal situation, their financial goals and some of the implications of their situation. Later in the process, these questions can then show the customer the benefits of taking action in order to meet their goals.

Here is a list of golden questions asked by some of the best digital, self-serve, financial planning services. These questions are given prior to the customer gaining a simple investment or pension fund strategy which seeks to address their needs. Typically, no more than one or two relevant questions are asked from a small number of categories:

1. Personal:
- Do you share your finances with a partner?
- How old are you?
- What rate of tax do you pay?

2. Goals:
- What do you want to achieve (e.g. retire, pay school fees, grow wealth, generate income)?
- How much will this cost?
- When?

3. Current financial arrangements:
- What's the current value of your investments?
- How much do you want to invest?
- Where are you invested today (cash, stocks, bonds, equities or more detailed asset allocation)?
- How much do you earn and how much do you spend?
- How much do you own (e.g. property) and how much do you owe (e.g. mortgage)?

4. Risk:
- What is your attitude to investment risk?
- What is your level of investment experience and engagement?
- What is your capacity to take on investment risk?
- What value are you prepared to put at risk?

Some use engaging graphics, some numbers, some just words, but all keep questions small, easy to understand

and easy to answer. The good digital services then let the engine do the work in the background and provide an initial sighting-shot of the implications of the customer's situation. For example, say the customer is 40 years old and wants to retire aged 65 on £45,000 a year and they have £50,000 invested in a pension today and a cautious attitude to risk. The asset and risk model can then show the customer: the likely range of incomes they might achieve in retirement, the likelihood of meeting their goal, in this case unlikely, and what actions they would need to take in order to do so; for example, investing more, taking more risk or postponing retirement. With good tools the user can then play with the key inputs and look at the impact on their situation. The adjustment process is key and is one of the most effective methods early in the process of gaining engagement. For example, letting the customer select a level of risk and see the impact on their potential investment returns and losses helps them better understand the impact of their choices and assess their chance of meeting goals.

This approach of asking simple questions upfront mimics what good advisers already do. They talk to customers and ask them, early on and in conversational terms, simple questions as part of the engagement and qualification process. They use their experience to circumvent the need to ask lots of detailed personal questions before establishing the customers' needs and whether in principle they can help. Good advisers provide feedback and some value-added insights to help the customer think about their situation in a helpful way. Assuming the customer is engaged, this is then followed up by an investment process which covers the necessary ground to ensure that the adviser really knows enough

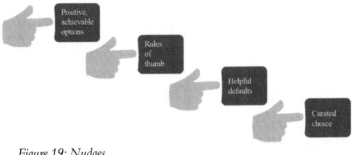

Figure 19: Nudges

about their customer and that any recommendations are suitable and compliant.

Technique 2: Positive financial nudges.

One of the challenges in helping a customer engage with financial planning is that as they begin to understand more about what is required to meet their goals, they lose heart as it all looks too difficult. In particular, for many who want to achieve financial security in retirement this often seems like an impossible task. Saying to the 40 year old with £50,000 in their pension, "You need to save £1 million in order to generate an income of £45,000 a year," is unlikely to generate a positive response. Put it another way though: "If you were to save ten percent of your income each month into a pension, increasing this a little above inflation each year in a medium-risk investment, and retire a little later, you could be most of the way towards maintaining your standard of living." Then you can get an entirely different and more engaged response.

You don't need to explain the benefits of grossing up, compounding, employer matching, escalating savings rates, state pension and drawdown, but focus on simple steps that feel achievable and that the client can say 'yes' to. The technical detail is important, but it only works if the customer feels that they can psychologically invest in the end result and that it is simple to take action. Positive nudges are a great way of making good choices more easily understandable and ultimately actionable.

Technique 3: Rules of thumb

With Pension Freedoms, the flexibility to produce income in retirement which doesn't rely on the one-off purchase of an annuity is now possible. Post-age-55 customers can, for example, access tax-free and taxable lump sums, draw down income for a period and then have a lump sum left in reserve for later life expenses, passing on to family or indeed buying an annuity. Explaining these choices in an engaging and understandable way and building a strategy around them is challenging. This is where rules of thumb can be helpful as simple principles which are generally reliable in the absence of full advice, to give broad steers on how to achieve a financial goal. In the context of a FinTech-supported planning service, they act as good starting points from which alternatives can be explored.

When it comes to retirement strategy, successful services use rules of thumb to set default planning assumptions for drawdown or annuity rates, for example. Without an expert's understanding of what is possible, customers left to their own devices in setting future-looking assumptions will struggle. DT completed a study in 2016 looking at the long-term impact of drawing down four percent a year at different risk levels. The study showed that if you used four percent as a rule of thumb then over the last ten years, customers would have maintained their capital on a total returns basis across all invested risk profiles except Risk Profile 1 (cash). While four percent may not be right for everyone, if the customer has a suitable risk profile then helping them understand a historically safe level of withdrawal will help them see how much they might access as income as a starting point in any plan while preserving their capital.

Showing a customer the range of potential outcomes that their investment may experience at a particular risk level based on defaults will also help them understand not only the level of investment they can withdraw but also what the 'journey' may be like along the way. Single deterministic illustration rates, as set out in pension statements, do not do the same thing. If anything, they run the risk of anchoring customers' expectations around unrealistic outcomes. If a customer has an equity portfolio it will not grow at a static annual percentage; it is much more likely to fluctuate within a range, growing on average over the longterm. Helping customers understand the range of returns in which an investment might operate say 90 percent of the time again helpfully sets expectations.

Providing a rule of thumb around inflation is also helpful in encouraging customer engagement with long-term planning. In 2001, the Government asked Ron Sandler[43] to look at the retail investment market and recommend policy responses to ensure that consumers were well served. Sandler concluded that many investors were being "recklessly conservative", keeping their money in bank or building society cash deposits and not taking enough risk to achieve the long-term, inflation-beating returns they need to achieve financial security in retirement. This problem persists today and in a low-returns environment where inflation remains a factor is arguably more acute.

Good digital services use simple rules of thumb around inflation to their advantage, showing what would happen to a customer's savings pot if they were left in a cash account and inflation were to operate at say 2.5 percent over the longterm. The real value of money saved in this way can be expected on average to decline over time and for someone who expects to be in retirement for several decades the uncomfortable implications of this 'do nothing' scenario can act as a powerful spur to action.

Technique 4: Curated choice

Finally, if you have helped your customer understand a suitable level of savings or withdrawals and the level of risk that is right for them, then providing them with a smaller, curated selection of good investment choices which meet their risk profile and objectives makes it easier for the customer to make a logical choice and take positive action. Operating long lists or building advisory or discretionary portfolios (except for the very highest-net-worth clients) is not only a complex, expensive and risky thing to do, but when it comes to a digital service for those seeking advice, it makes their job harder. In a digital service, the user-experience experts would call this 'increased cognitive load', i.e. the amount of thinking the user must do. As shown in the California jam study, while choice initially seems attractive, fewer customers take action in this scenario, compared to a smaller number of considered pre-configured options. Over the last few years, risk-profiled and risk-targeted funds or portfolios have emerged as a powerful way of curating choice for customers in this situation. Successful digital services, be they adviser-driven or customer-led, are increasingly adopting this kind of curation to help customers and their advisers make good and suitable choices.

Best-practice learnings

- Successful firms recognise that financial planning is a challenge because it requires slow, thoughtful thinking which most people find hard. They also acknowledge that most customers are risk averse, lack trust in financial services and find the complexity and range of choice available off-putting
- As a result, they recognise their role as a 'choice architect' deliberately making it easier to engage with the financial planning process through golden questions, positive nudges and rules of thumb
- Successful financial planning services the world over increasingly use FinTech to curate simpler, more transparent options, basing these around the customer's objectives and risk profile so they find it easier to make better choices and to act

How to bring advisers with you

This chapter looks at:

- How intelligent technology is being adopted in other industries and the insights this offers for financial planning and financial advisers
- Why advisers are often concerned about the use of FinTech in the planning process
- How businesses who successfully adopt FinTech engage advisers and keep them on board

There are different levels of automation in the car industry. Level 1 includes cruise control, level 2 includes adaptive cruise control or lane changing where the car undertakes a specific task but where the human driver is still responsible for monitoring the driving environment, right up to level 5 where the car is completely autonomous and there is no expectation that a human will intervene as the car takes you safely from point A to B and back again. At the time of publishing there are no commercially available level 3 cars, where the car does most of the driving, monitoring the environment for you and driving accordingly but a human can take over. Many commentators expect level 3 cars to become commercially available over the next few years while several of the big manufacturers like Ford are targeting 2021 and beyond for levels 4 and 5. These manufacturers see a safer world with fewer—if any—accidents, and a world in which taxi services could run continuously 24 hours a day without a driver, significantly reducing the cost of travel as a car can then make money at any time of day or night, rather than standing idle outside a driver's house for much of the time.

Investment advisers and planners are often concerned that the use of technology will devalue their role or somehow make the customer feel that they can do what the adviser is doing. Unfortunately, as a result many advisers still use paper factfinds and paper-based risk profiling with their clients and avoid using planning tools or any FinTech in front of clients. If all the adviser is doing is product and fund-picking for their client and pitting their knowledge of investments against the customer's—then there may be some truth in this; after all, many sources of fund information and guidance are readily available online for free. Picking funds is very like undertaking a level 1 driving automation task in that it is not a task that takes account of the environment. In the case of financial planning, the environment is the customer's situation, their evolving needs and the lifestyle and goals they want to have in a future which is uncertain. This is the challenge for financial planning as I set out in Chapter 1: building a long-term plan which helps the customer meet their future goals, in a manner that is suitable to their circumstance at a cost and risk that is *right for them*.

Advisers provide value and engagement through the

consultative, empathetic approach that only they as human beings can bring to illicit an understanding of the customer. This is in addition to the trust that stems from their technical knowledge and experience. Technical answers to most financial planning questions can be found online. It's the questions about what is suitable for the customer and their circumstances that aren't, along with judgement based on experience of the right approach from the myriad options that customers face. Advisers often bring decades of training, knowledge and experience in:

- Helping customers uncover and articulate what their goals and concerns really are
- Converting anecdotal thoughts and feelings into a risk-based plan
- Selecting suitable investments, products and tax wrappers to support the plan
- Managing those solutions to ensure they deliver against the plan on an ongoing basis and *providing reassurance to the customer along the way*

Technology cannot yet provide empathy, the motivation to act, or the trust and confidence that you are doing the right thing for yourself in an area in which most consumers have low confidence, little experience and low levels of engagement. Professional financial planning will offer a long and healthy career path for many decades ahead in combination with the right FinTech.

One of my favourite quotes in relation to the use of automation this time in the airline industry is from Patrick Smith, a veteran pilot, in his book Cockpit Confidential[44];:"One of the most stubborn myths in all of aviation is this notion that pilots just sit there while the plane flies itself from City A to City B. It's infuriating to know that people believe this, because it's utterly false. Airplanes do not fly themselves. The crew flies the airplane through the automation. A plane cannot fly itself any more than an operating room, with all of its advanced technical equipment, is able to perform an organ transplant by itself. The equipment makes things easier, but the operation itself is controlled by humans."

"The crew flies the airplane through the automation". This is the way that I believe financial advisers should view FinTech today and for some years to come. It provides automation which helps you deliver parts of the financial planning process faster, with less cost, less risk and a greater consistency of outcome than completing the task manually. Over time of course automation will become more sophisticated and will be able to handle more and more complex environments. It will free up professional advisers to work more closely with clients in areas where greater empathy and expertise is required and valued.

Other professions are embracing technology in a similar fashion to reduce the time, cost and risk required of highly qualified professionals while increasing digital access to elements of their services. In medicine GPs have for many years used practice management systems and web-based diagnostic systems in their offices. They have now started making variations of these systems available online direct to patients for them to get help and guidance faster. In the field of law, online dispute resolution platforms have been widely used in the US and by companies such as eBay, for example, to help online buyers and sellers across Europe settle disputes without face-to-face mediation and the involvement of highly qualified and costly professionals.

The financial advice firms I have worked with who have most successfully brought advisers on side—and got them excited about the use of FinTech in the planning process—have had the following in common. They:

- Give advisers a clear understanding of how *their* world will be better and answer the 'what's in it for me?' question. It might be the ability to acquire or see more customers and make more money, or it may be to reduce the amount of painful administration or desk-based analysis which are the bane of many advisers' lives.
- Show how the service will make the adviser look good in the customer's eyes. This might be as simple as a professional risk profiling or asset allocation report or it might be an ongoing service built around a digital app that tracks the customer's portfolio and its suitability. The adviser can see that the service will make them look good to their target customer base.
- Provide strong senior-level sponsorship, usually from the chief executive and board, who recognise that the business needs to adopt more technology in its financial planning processes and paint a clear vision.
- Demonstrate how customers will be better off and better served with the firm's proposition in a manner that is not possible currently. The firm's investment proposition is not surprisingly an area of great sensitivity and so a vision which shows how this can be embedded in the technology and delivered successfully and not contorted is high on the priority list for many advisers.
- Build close working relationships between management and one or more influential and innovative advisers in the business, who can see the benefits and are keen to

utilise more technology and to whom others will listen. In a small firm this can be one and the same person!

- Gain support from administration and compliance people who ideally will need the planning technology integrated into their back office systems and processes so that it does not generate additional work downstream and makes their lives easier.
- Invest in the training and roll out of the technology, providing plenty of time to inform and educate advisers, with ongoing support; often using online webinars and phone rather than having to pull advisers off the road for extensive periods.
- Select technology which is easy to learn and easy to use. Advisers in businesses small and large don't want an extra piece of technology in their lives unless it meets these criteria.

Financial advisers who have successfully engaged with digital see that their role is not diminished through its use, but quite the reverse: it helps them deliver good outcomes for more customers on a consistent basis, with less work, less risk and more profit.

Best-practice learnings

- Firms which successfully embrace FinTech accept that there is a difference between automating tasks and the empathy required to understand a customer's situation and build a plan on which the customer is willing to take action
- Successful firms are ones that sponsor adoption of technology from the top and have a clear vision for

not just the benefits to customers but the benefits to advisers, administrators, compliance and other key stakeholders too–they answer the 'what's in it for me?' question

- The embedding of a firm's investment proposition is an area of particular sensitivity. Ensuring that this is well supported and delivered at lower cost and risk will be a big win

Managing systemic risk

This chapter looks at:

- Why the application of rule or model-driven advice creates the potential for systemic risk
- The compliance benefits of using model-driven systems and the benefits of using an independent model
- Three rules for managing systemic risk, particularly as greater degrees of automation are applied
- How to protect vulnerable customers who need more support than an automated process can provide

Current UK compliance infrastructure is based on the manual provision of advice by advisers. The application of FinTech means changing these processes and systems whether that is a little, for example through the use of a digital risk-profiling process, or more substantially through the application of automation in a customer-facing advice process. While the opportunities flowing from the use of FinTech in the advice process are significant, the consequences of getting it wrong could also be severe—on the customer and the firm—because if you deliver your service at scale using digital, any problems could magnify quickly. If advice is unsuitable for one customer with a particular set of circumstances, using a certain set of rules, it could also be wrong for all customers advised in the same way. Delivering unsuitable advice means potential customer redress, and sanctions by the FCA and potentially the Financial Ombudsman Service.

That said, accurately calibrated and comprehensively tested FinTech systems, driven by advisers or by customers, will deliver more consistent answers compared to manual approaches. This will reduce the variability of your financial planning and advice. They also will deliver a level of transparency and auditability which manual advice processes and 'the conversation on the couch' cannot. This chapter looks at the three rules firms who have successfully applied greater degrees of automation have used to ensure good management of the risks.

Before looking at these rules though, it's worth focusing on the importance and value of using an independent model rather than a bespoke solution built solely for your own customer base. As discussed in Chapter 8, over the last decade there has been a revolution in UK financial planning with the adoption of model-driven, risk-profiling and asset-allocation tools. Ten years ago, the use of tools was very limited, with 80 percent of firms adopting a manual, home-grown approach. Today most firms use a digital service as part of their process. In the early years, many of these tools were accessed via life companies and investment product providers, who funded them and, to a greater or lesser degree, used them to support the sale of their own investment propositions.

After the Retail Distribution Review and the banning of commission both hard, by way of remuneration, and soft in terms of dependency on product provider systems, the industry has come to realise that the independence and objectivity of an asset and risk model is key to ensuring that a customer is treated fairly and without bias. The less obvious, but increasingly important, benefit has been to produce much larger *industrywide* data sets with more accurate calibration of models than a sole company with a single customer base can achieve on its own. This 'big data' is now coming into its own as a means of testing greater degrees of automation without live running.

The three rules that firms follow to best manage the risk associated with a digital service are:

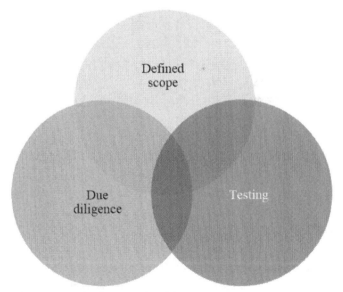

Figure 20: 3 rules for managing risk

Rule 1: Clearly define the scope of your service

Firstly, they clearly define the scope of their service in the context of a specific target audience. Whether this is the introduction of a risk-profiling service for use by advisers or a fully-fledged automated advice service used directly by customers, being clear on both scope and target audience is critical.

The setting of the scope of any service has a direct impact on your firm's responsibilities. These responsibilities are based on "the nature and extent of the service to be provided and the type of product or transaction envisaged, including their complexity and the risks involved" according to the FCA Handbook 9.2.2[45]. As a result, generally speaking, the more automated the service, the more a narrower scope is helpful. A narrower scope enables the organisation to be very clear on what it includes and what it excludes as well as who the service is aimed at and who should not use it. For example, does the service cover advice on investing cash only or does it look at existing investments? Does it cover investment into only a single product type, for example, a Stocks and Shares ISA or a personal pension, or does it give product advice across a range of products for a range of financial needs? Is it a one-off service or is it an ongoing review part of the service? Is it restricted to a single product range or does it provide advice on products from across the whole of the market?

With a narrower scope of service, it is a more straightforward job to ensure it is appropriately targeted. For example, if a customer is approaching retirement and looking for a general review of their finances, then advice only on investing cash into a stocks and shares ISA would be unlikely to be appropriate. Firms offering holistic reviews through automation often find themselves having to capture significantly more data than narrower, more targeted services; the result is that these services quickly become less appealing to customers.

Rule 2: Due diligence—understand your asset and risk model

Secondly, successful firms understand the core asset and risk model they have adopted, its strengths and limitations and complete their due diligence on it. Given that models are representations of reality and make approximations and assumptions, they all have limitations. Successful firms recognise this and understand the key assumptions being made, particularly those around the long-term returns, volatilities and correlations. They ask for the documentation and sense-check this against other approaches. They also ask questions about how the asset allocations have performed historically versus their forecasts. They understand how often assumptions are updated and what the process is for doing so—is it rigorous, does it have external review from an independent investment committee or similar governance?

The key is to be able to check that assumptions are reasoned and reasonable and that you can explain the main ones to your customers so that they too can understand them. Look at the asset allocations at each risk level, because these will be central drivers of any financial planning or, in a more automated service, advice. Do they represent a smooth gradient from cash through to emerging markets, so that you can fairly compare what the customer has today without contorting their position? Some models only cover the mid-range of investment risks. It's impossible to show a customer where they are today if their savings are mostly in a bank account and your risk spectrum doesn't start at cash.

When you are implementing your digital service, your philosophy should be *customer first*, not product first. In a smaller firm this often comes quite naturally; you are at the sharp end of dealing with customers every day. In a larger firm, with different teams responsible for customer relationships, investment strategy and product selection, it is critical that your assumptions and model are built from the 'outside in', not from the 'inside out'. Let the customer-facing and investment teams do their work first, before thinking, 'What product do I want to sell most?' and then using a model to make these look good.

Rule 3: Rigorous testing

Thirdly, testing the service to ensure it is suitable for your target customer group is key. The extent of any testing should in part be a function of the level of automation being introduced. The introduction of a new risk-profiling process at one level could potentially be done by running it in parallel with an existing process for a short period, checking that outcomes are as expected or if they differ noting as to why. For more automated systems working through expected and actual outcomes for customers with different risk profiles, portfolio sizes, goals and needs will help ensure the service has been calibrated properly for your organisation. The more automated the service, the more you need to test outcomes in each of these different areas and ensure they are as expected.

The FCA is rightly concerned about vulnerable

customers in society. These include those with long-term or significant illness, carers, older people, those who are unemployed or have suffered a job loss, those with low basic skills or those who have been bereaved. In a traditional face-to-face advice scenario, these areas would typically be discussed as part of a fact find of softer facts and understanding of the customer's current circumstances. A qualified adviser's training, empathy and experience will typically help assess and handle the vulnerability appropriately. Where a service is more automated it is important to recognise according to FCA research[46] that vulnerable customers can often utilise online channels because it minimises or avoids human interaction, which in their particular circumstances they may find easier and more expedient rather than discussing their situation with a human adviser. They may perceive that a discussion with a human might result in an alternative course of action, for example, not to take on the risk of investing–in this case ensuring that any automated service provides clear access and signposting to human contact at appropriate points and where there are any potential affordability or capacity issues which could constrain the customer's ability to invest for the longterm that they are guided to talk to an adviser rather than completing the process online.

In any test case defining a 'good financial planning outcome' is key. Good outcomes are subjective and having a range of qualified and experienced individuals contributing to what good looks like given specific customer needs is without doubt the most effective way of creating test strategies. These might include experienced financial advisers and experts from compliance and investment management.

Some firms start testing the service 'in a corner of the business' on a small number of customers before rolling out more widely. Some have tested the service on their staff first and then customers prior to a wider roll-out. Some dual-run the new digital service with existing processes to compare the results for a period. It's important, from a treating customers fairly perspective, to know how they will receive your advice. The more you apply automation, the more important testing of outcomes is.

It is worth focusing on Simplified Advice here, because this is the form of streamlining the Regulator is focusing on to encourage wider adoption and this is the approach that most organisations worldwide are having most success with. Simplified Advice[47] was introduced in March 2012 by the FSA. While not a defined term in the Handbook, it has been adopted to describe streamlined advice processes which aim to address straightforward needs of consumers. In essence, it takes Focused Advice, where the customer at their instigation requests that their adviser addresses only certain needs, and provides a framework for assessing simple investment needs. It doesn't involve detailed analysis of the customer's circumstances that are not directly relevant to those needs. Once you have set your scope, to ensure your service delivers the compliance benefits that digital can bring you need to design, build and test a process and outputs which ensure the following:

- Customers understand the limitations and boundaries, and don't just 'click through' warnings in a way they don't engage with them
- The service undertakes a robust gating to ensure the service is suitable within the boundaries you set; for example, you don't necessarily rely on the customer's own judgement that their current level of expenditure is affordable

- Vulnerable customers or customers who are not suitable for the service or who may not understand it are directed to speak to an adviser
- You actively mitigate any limitations of the tool; for example, checking for contradictory answers and playing back responses for client confirmation

While not an exhaustive list, clients who have implemented self-serve digital services have had positive experiences when working with FCA Project Innovate to work through the above.

The FCA have also published guidance on good and bad practice for streamlined advice services[48], a summary checklist of which can be found in the appendix to this book.

Best-practice learnings

- Clearly define the scope of any digital service to ensure it's appropriate for your target audience
- Perform due diligence and understand the strengths and limitations of your model as this will be the engine which drives your advice
- Where possible utilise an independent model which will benefit from data and insights from a wider customer base than in-house
- Test the service prior to rolling it out, or ask your service provider for their test results and then roll out slowly, initially perhaps on staff and a small number of customers, before wider roll-out

Building bridges between data islands

This chapter looks at:

- The often fragmented systems which sit in the back offices of financial advice firms large and small
- The challenge these data islands create for firms in terms of automation and ability to scale
- Why an integrated best-of-breed approach to the key systems in your business will deliver greatest benefits in the short and long term

A few years ago I drove out to the countryside and parked outside an anonymous, grey, 1950s, breeze-block building. I was welcomed inside and offered coffee. While I waited, I took in my surroundings: wall upon wall of beige hanging files all with private client fact finds, illustrations, application forms, correspondence and paperwork, and an army of administrators photocopying, stapling, scanning and talking on the phone. There were several fax machines on display. That morning I was given a tour of the systems used including:

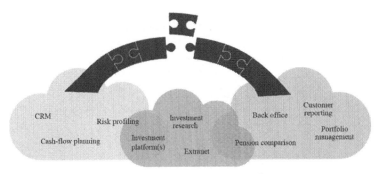

Figure 21: Building bridges

1. Customer relationship management (CRM)
2. Back office commissions / adviser charging
3. Risk profiling
4. Cash-flow planning
5. Pension and product comparison
6. Investment research
7. Customer reporting
8. Investment platforms
9. Providers' extranets
10. Portfolio management

Each system required a separate process and careful training, and no system talked to another—each was an island. Re-keying client data from one to another was the norm. Welcome to the back office of one of the country's largest private client IFAs.

Retail financial services is a complex, highly regulated and rapidly changing market with a significant number of niches and variations in advice models. From a technology point of view, the result is lots of systems with many different specialisations. This is not helpful when it comes to digitising some or all the financial planning process, because each system can be an island of data. The pain caused by data islands is significant and can be summarised in two ways.

Issue 1: Cost and inability to automate

It's difficult to automate a process when your data sits in different systems. The most common workaround is to re-key data from one to another and, needless to say, this is labour intensive and runs the risk of errors being introduced during the process. I once met a firm who had reached the point of actually accruing for the financial redress they expected to have to make as a result of errors generated during the portfolio rebalancing process each quarter. Regardless of the checks they put in place, the precision required to review and rebalance large numbers of portfolios was too difficult for people to get right. They recognised that this was not a sustainable situation and that the number of customers they could serve was being heavily constrained. In fact, they were at a point where for every few customers they took on they had to think about taking on more administration staff. As a result, their revenues and profits were static and their ability to serve and access more customers was severely constrained.

This experience is borne out in an independent study commissioned from the Financial & Technology Research Centre (F&TRC)[49] on building a robust and efficient investment review process. The study estimated the average time to complete a single investment review was six hours of adviser and administrator time using typical manual, unintegrated processes and systems. Much of this time was spent obtaining valuations from platforms and providers, creating a review report based on asset allocation information from fact sheets, risk profiling the client from a paper questionnaire, recommending an investment strategy and then transacting the recommendation by manually keying onto an investment platform. This picture is clearly not one of a slick, automated, scalable process but it still is one that is commonly found across the industry. Looking at the economics of an unintegrated process, on average six hours of qualified adviser time should be charged out at least at £900 assuming a desire to make a 20 percent+ profit margin after adviser salary and overheads. This works if the client has a portfolio of more than £180,000 and is willing and able to pay 0.5 percent a year in fees (or £90,000 if they are willing to pay one percent), but if they are not then the process becomes very expensive indeed and profit margins reduced. The result is that many financial advice firms have moved out of the mass market, because most customers don't have portfolios of this size to invest. According to HM Treasury only nine percent of people in the UK have more than £100,000 to invest (excluding pensions). However, 24 percent have between £10,000 and £99,000 of savings or investable assets. Profitable access to these customers is prohibited because of the cost and expense of current advice processes because of systems and data islands that don't talk to each other.

Issue 2: Loss of asset and risk model integrity

The second issue caused by data islands is that of losing asset and risk model integrity. Building an investment recommendation based on data held in a back office, platform or portfolio-management system is challenging because of the different data definitions and accuracy of these systems.

ARM integrity, the backbone of suitability, relies on consistent definitions of asset classes, their risk and return parameters, risk profiles and covariances. Accurately transposing data from multiple sources even for a single portfolio is laborious and prone to error. More fundamentally, it's simply not possible to achieve an accurate translation of one asset class definition to another for many types of assets, for example, international equities or bonds, because the underlying definitions are frequently not readily available and nor are the individual holdings within a fund. As data is re-keyed from one system to another without reference to a consistent and accurate definition integrity is broken.

Loss of ARM integrity also makes customer servicing more challenging, because assessment of portfolio drift or performance in relation to the customer's planned risk profile needs to accurately reflect the definitions used with the customer to create their plan in the first place. The more automated the service, the more consistency of reference data matters.

Financial institutions and vendors have tried to deliver good end-to-end enterprise systems over the last decade and have spent many tens of millions of pounds in doing so. However, in a rapidly evolving market, the cost and specialist skills required to have a strong application which covers the whole waterfront from front to back office have proven too challenging. Even in much larger markets, such as the US, the same fragmented pattern exists because of the specialist skills and technology required in each part of the planning process. For example, to deliver risk-profiling and financial planning services you need qualified financial planning, Chartered Financial Analyst, investment research, actuarial and mathematical resources, as well as core usability and software development skills. These are not needed in CRM, back office or platform teams.

The most effective answer or system architecture is the integration of best-of-breed systems, each strong in their own domain, with clarity around which set of data is owned or mastered where and an agreed set of reference data.

The best examples are where three or four core system types support a joined-up service with:

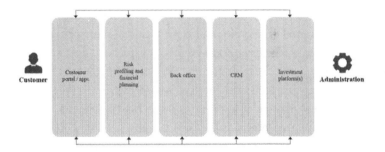

Figure 22: Best-practice systems architecture

- CRM owning basic details around the customer, their marketing and communications
- Back office owning financials, fees, compliance (this may be the same as the CRM in an IFA practice) and workflow
- A smaller number of platforms or a portfolio-management system mastering portfolio information
- A specialist risk-profiling and financial planning system supporting the planning and advice process. It pulls data for the profiling, planning, portfolio construction and monitoring process and pushes transaction requests and enriched data back to the CRM/back office and/or platforms
- A customer-facing portal or app which aggregates

portfolio data including off platform assets and tracks performance against the financial plan and risk profile. It draws its data from the back office and/or financial planning system. The portal enables secure communication between the adviser and the customer and is the access point for customer facing tools and automated advice services

A joined-up approach which removes re-keying and ensures ARM integrity radically reduces the time, cost and risk of planning and servicing customers. The study from the F&TRC showed a *700 percent improvement* in productivity, reducing the six hours eight minutes for an investment review to 49 minutes when integrated. A saving of five hours nine minutes per case. The report summarised: "Put in other terms an adviser would be able to complete more than seven times as many reviews using a joined-up process as they would have when using a manual paper based process. This means that the costs of providing on-going services to clients could be reduced and services could be provided to clients where costs were previously a barrier."

A joined-up approach also helps ensure ARM integrity and ongoing suitability, and forms the basis of an efficient data flow which can be accessed by a customer facing portal or app and more automated, customer-facing digital services.

A by-product of this approach is also likely to be increased customer satisfaction and retention, as customers can access their portfolio and see how it's tracking against the risk profile and plan agreed. Further support for a valuable financial planning service for which customers are happy to pay.

Best-practice learnings

- The complexity of retail financial services drives system specialisation with firms that excel in each. The best strategy is to work with best of breed and bridge data islands through two-way integrations
- Ensure asset model integrity by using reference data from your investment planning process throughout the customer journey. Think *customer* plan, not product plan
- Use the planning process to build bridges between data islands. Specialist risk profiling and planning systems pull data from multiple sources, enrich it through the planning process and then push it back to the back office and platforms as systems of record

Section 4:

Catching the wave

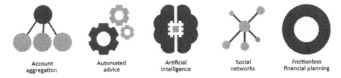

Figure 23: 5 future developments that will change the game

Future game changers

This book is all about the digital wave that's starting to crash across the industry now, and how financial advice firms can take advantage of the opportunities FinTech offers today. You don't need a crystal ball to see what others are already doing and how to take advantage of this for your own business. The adoption of FinTech in financial planning will, however, revolutionise the industry over the long term and so this chapter picks out the five big trends that are likely to change the game and how to start future proofing your business.

Account aggregation

As I pointed out in Chapter 8 one of the barriers to greater automation is access to the large amounts of data needed to advise a customer. Without this data, the advice process takes a long time; automated or otherwise. Over time, improved aggregation of financial arrangements data and its access by both advisers and customers will change this.

Account aggregation has been available in the US since 1999 via firms like Yodlee[50] and Mint[51] and in the UK for at least a decade with services like Sammedia[52] for IFAs and Money Dashboard[53]. It hasn't gone mainstream in the UK for several reasons: security concerns, lack of support from financial services companies and perhaps a particularly ingrained approach to 'mental accounting' where different pots of money are mentally and physically kept in different places. However, this will undoubtedly change over time as it has done in the US, with improvements in aggregation services and the adoption of this kind of technology by larger wealth managers and banks. FCA's Project Innovate and Government initiatives such as the Pensions Dashboard[54], recognise the importance of giving people a clear understanding of their current arrangements as a platform for improving their finances and this will help drive change too.

Once customers and advisers have access to accurate, up-to-date financial arrangement data, as they have with online banking for example, behaviours are likely to change. Customers could be expected to monitor their balances more often, improve their understanding of their arrangements and seek advice, so long as it is accessible, more frequently. A report from the British Bankers Association in 2015[55] showed the number of people physically going into branches had fallen by around 30 percent in the previous three years, while at the same time banks had begun to send many millions of text message alerts to customers each week signalling their proximity to pre-set balance limits, showing what can be done, once you have accurate data.

What can you do about this now? Make the most of your position as a financial advice firm and your agency code. Use the aggregation capabilities available in your back office or financial planning service to add value to your customer proposition with this powerful approach. Independent advisers are in a unique position to be able to offer customers a 360 degree perspective on their wealth and assets—providing a breakdown and commentary on their products, asset allocation, the risk they are taking and where there are concentrations of assets or products which could be diversified.

Simple, automated advice

Simple, regulated, automated advice delivered as part of a hybrid model and which is sufficiently personalised will without doubt be a game changer when delivered well and through trusted advisers and/or brands. As I set out in Chapter 9, over the next few years, assuming the Government and Regulator continue to encourage it, automated advice will move from provision through a few innovative early adopters, into the mainstream. Its effect will be revolutionary. Most customers have quite simple needs and questions most of the time. Simple, automated services are well placed to answer these questions and when delivered well as part of a hybrid model where customers can talk to an adviser or representative they trust, the take-up can be expected to be substantial. For advisers and firms, it will enable them to start to build (or rebuild) relationships with customers with smaller balances; for consumers it will provide easy access to the key questions they need answering from people they trust. The largest Registered Investment Adviser in the US is Financial Engines which advises on well over $1 trillion for 900 million employees[56].

They use automated advice online backed up by telephone agents and advisers. In 2016, they bought a chain of high street investment advisers who will provide advice based on Financial Engines' algorithms.

What can you do about this today? Evaluate the range of automation solutions available on the market today from service providers. Depending on the size and sophistication of your firm you may want to take a solution off the shelf, of which there are a number to choose from, or build from scratch from components. DigitalWealthInsights.com is a service that has been created for professionals who want to understand more about the digital wealth management market both in the UK and globally[57].

Social networks

In Chapter 12 I looked at the potential impact of social networks and large numbers of consumers sharing their financial plans to gain help, guidance or advice from people like them. Of all the developments on the horizon, this one has the potential to be most disruptive, particularly given its currently unregulated nature. Through a community of 'people like you', the ability to gain feedback on investments and strategies is already possible. Sites like Motif Investing[58] and eToro[59] are built around the concept of social investing and the ability for users to explicitly watch other investors' strategies, to discuss and copy them. They benefit from the wisdom of crowds and of highly rated individuals and break down the traditional information imbalance between professionals and customers.

While this approach has yet to make it to mainstream UK retail investing, you only have to look at the discussion boards of firms like moneysavingexpert.com or Interactive Investor[60] where community members give their opinions on individual investments' strengths and weaknesses to see thriving communities helping each other.

So, what should your firm do today? When financial communities move mainstream, it will be important for financial advisers and institutions to be participating in them, engaging via social media and expending effort to manage and develop their digital reputation. Social media will break down the one-to-one relationship advisers have with clients and it will be important to be part of these networks and conversations.

Artificial intelligence

One of the significant side effects of the above trends is the creation of huge amounts of accurate data. Accuracy is important because historically advisers have had to rely on snapshots of data, very often manually updated as and when through their back office. The quality of this data means it's difficult to see accurate patterns, particularly over time, let alone to build reliable models of consumer behaviour. Once the accuracy problem is solved, however, then building predictive models becomes possible. Imagine having aggregated data on a customer and applying planning algorithms which make recommendations that are not only suitable but, based on data, more likely to be adopted by the customer such that they take action and *stay the course over time*. Predictive models will help firms provide advice, guidance and marketing promotions. They will enable organisations to target messages based on customer demographics and social media activity, the performance of markets or asset classes and the movement of individual portfolios or financial arrangements relative to goals. At one end of the spectrum asset managers could, for example, run targeted marketing to advisers and customers based on their propensity or likelihood to take particular actions; inputs might well include data from social media activity as above. On a more personalised basis, guidance or advice messages could be aimed at clients not just based on probabilistic financial planning models as they are now, but based on artificial intelligence assessing the experience of large numbers of similar consumers who have taken similar actions in the past, perhaps driven by automated advice, and either met or not met their desired outcomes.

What should firms do today? Maximise the use of the CRM capabilities you have in your systems and think of ways to personalise communications with your customers. From simple campaigns based on tax year end or birthdays, to more sophisticated campaigns based on risk profiles or asset allocations, learning how to maximise the insights your data can give you will stand your firm in good stead. For larger firms, services provided by Amazon[61] or Microsoft's Machine Learning Studio[62] make it easier for you to build models that generate insights from your data.

Frictionless financial planning

There have been many, many attempts to bring holistic financial planning mainstream online, including our own at Sort back in 2000. The challenges though are immense, not least the need to create a frictionless experience for the customer in an area where, as I set out in Chapter 9, there are significant levels of inertia. But in the same way that healthtech is allowing consumers to set goals, monitor their calorific inputs and outputs (food and exercise) using wearables, gain encouragement from communities of likeminded people and receive nudges and advice based on AI algorithms, you can imagine the same in personal finance. The power of this approach comes not just in the automation of advice but in the automation of feedback and adjustment based on what the customer actually experiences. In the same way that Waze[63] revolutionised the satnav world by providing real-time feedback on traffic flows from other mobile devices, feedback from other people like you on the same journey towards, say retirement, could be massively appealing to consumers as well as massively disruptive for the traditional professional advice industry if advisers aren't part of it.

How should firms position themselves today? If you're not using risk-based cashflow planning today then it's a great start. Unlike deterministic planning (where investments are assumed to grow at fixed rates—which they don't), building risk-based cashflow plans based on your customers' risk profile and their goals, fed by accurate data from account aggregation, provides a strong basis for an enduring relationship.

Conclusions

Catching and riding the digital financial planning wave with FinTech as it grows and swells offers huge opportunities. For large institutions, get it right and your brand and channel presence can take a well-designed, well-executed service to millions more customers who were previously uneconomic. For smaller firms, digital offers you the opportunity to scale and become more profitable beyond that which was traditionally possible. For all firms, the four big opportunities digital offers are:

- Massively growing your firm's productivity, reducing your cost to serve and increasing your profits
- Transforming access to your advice and planning services
- Enhancing services so you can retain and grow customers who will be only too happy to pay your fees
- Reducing your compliance risk by building suitability into your firm's DNA

As I have shown, running a manual business in a digital world is already a risky proposition, and with the first waves of the tsunami of change already lapping over the industry, now is the time to change! From the introduction of 'premium calculators' on basic laptops for a few salespeople in the 1980s to today where the Treasury and FCA are championing the use of FinTech to support access to advice for mainstream consumers, you can see the pace of change is only accelerating. It isn't stopping either; future developments like account aggregation, automated advice, artificial intelligence and social networks will change the game even faster enabling 'frictionless financial planning'.

I hope you find this book a valuable resource as you embark on your own voyage. If you want to know more about FinTech in risk profiling and financial planning, review the latest industry developments or want to share your own experiences, visit www.dynamicplanner.com and don't hesitate to get in touch.

Best of luck!
Ben

Appendix I – FinTech financial planning service due diligence checklist

Below is a checklist based on this book which summarises the key areas to review when undertaking due diligence on a FinTech service for your business.

Question	Answer
Risk profiling, investment process and suitability	
1. Does the risk profiling service support:	
a. A scientifically proven psychometric questionnaire backed up by large data sets	
b. Effective assessment of investor experience and engagement	
c. Accurate assessment of risk capacity	

Question	Answer
d. Proven value-at-risk model, a long-term track record, including during pronounced bear markets	
2. Does the asset and risk model have integrity and consistency from investor to investments, including, clear:	
a. Risk definitions and boundaries?	
b. Asset class definitions and assumptions?	
c. Language from customer to investment manager?	
3. Does it have a published track record evidencing the asset model integrity?	
4. Is it self-explanatory and easy to relay to the end customer?	
5. Are investment solutions consistently aligned against specific risk targets or 'outcomes'? Can these outcomes be demonstrated at scale and over time?	

Question	Answer
6. Does the service provide a strong audit trail?	
7. Does the service support multiple channels for engaging customers—e.g. email, web link, web based and mobile app?	
8. Does the service provide a consistent and whole of market analysis of both your customer's existing and prospective investments?	
9. Does the service meet FCA best practice from FG2011/05?	
10. If used across multiple channels, does the service ensure a consistent approach to suitability across all channels?	

Question	Answer
Business model	
1. Does the service support sufficient levels of automation, from needs analysis and guidance, through personal recommendations for your business model and strategy?	
2. Does the service support a hybrid model which incorporates elements of customer self-serve in combination with adviser interaction?	
3. Can customer activity be tracked from one channel to another with full audit trail?	
4. Does the service provide digital outputs which can be easily shared and compared by customers on social media?	
5. Is the service flexible and does it allow you to update your investment proposition from time to time?	

Question	Answer
6. Does the service provide branded customer portals or apps for secure access and review on anytime, anywhere devices?	
Engaging customers digitally	
1. Have the outputs and reports been well designed? Will they make you and your advisers look good and build trust with customers? Are the outputs fair, clear and not misleading?	
2. Does the service provide an interactive and engaging process for your customers, including use of data-driven challenges around inconsistencies in customer answers?	
3. Does the service play back customer answers and add value by providing insights into their situation?	
4. Does it make use of:	
a. Golden questions	

Question	Answer
b. Positive financial nudges	
c. Rules of thumb	
d. Curated choice	
Bringing advisers with you	
1. Does the service answer the 'what's in it for me?' question?	
2. Does it demonstrate how customers will be served with your centralised investment proposition in a manner that is not possible currently?	
3. Are there strong training and adoption plans available with the service?	
4. Is the service easy to learn and easy to use?	
Managing your risk	
1. Is the scope of service clearly defined?	
2. Are the strengths and limitations made clear?	
3. Has rigorous testing been undertaken to show that:	

Question	Answer
a. Customers understand the limitations and boundaries and don't just click through warnings?	
b. Robust gating is in place to ensure the service is suitable within the boundaries you set and those for whom it is not suitable are gated out?	
c. Vulnerable customers or customers who are not suitable for the service or who may not understand it are directed to speak to an adviser.	
d. You actively mitigate any limitations of the tool; for example, checking for contradictory answers and playing back responses for client confirmation.	
Systems architecture	
1. Does the service talk to your other systems and bridge the data islands in your business?	

Question	Answer
2. Does the service allow you to take an integrated, best-of-breed approach?	
3. Does the service use data from your back office and platforms and push enriched data from the planning process and proposed transactions back to these systems?	
4. Has the service been subject to independent security testing?	
5. Has the service been subject to performance and load testing?	

Appendix 2 – Summary of FCA guidance on streamlined advice services

The following is a summary of the guidance on streamlined advice set out in the FCA Guidance Consultation, April 2017[64].

1. Who is the service aimed at?

Firms need to be clear on the nature of the clients at whom the service is aimed and their needs. Products to be distributed or advised on need to be suitable for these types of clients, as does the firm's marketing strategy, the design of the customer interface and the controls firms put in place to monitor the quality of client outcomes.

Firms should use their knowledge of their target clients to 'triage' or filter out those clients whose needs, characteristics and objectives are not compatible.

2. Ongoing monitoring of the use of their service

Firms should maintain ongoing monitoring of who is using the streamlined service and take action if consumers are receiving unsuitable personal recommendations or are outside their target market.

3. Design of client interface

This needs to have due regard to the information needs of clients, their likely level of financial knowledge and experience, and to communicate information in a way which is clear, fair and not misleading.

4. Product selection

Firms should not offer products through their streamlined advice services if there is an incompatibility between the target market for the products to be offered and the clients to whom the firm intends to promote its streamlined advice service. This could arise because of particular product characteristics such as:

- Minimum contribution rates – are they affordable for the firm's target clients?
- Access and flexibility – for example, do the firm's target clients need to be able to change contribution levels easily or switch products without penalty?
- The risk of each product, including the volatility and whether this is consistent with the typical risk and knowledge/experience profiles of the firm's target clients

5. Disclosing the nature of the service

Firms must disclose information about the nature and scope of the streamlined service being provided.

6. Client information and suitability

Firms must take reasonable steps to ensure that a personal recommendation is suitable for a client. These include assessing the client's:

- Knowledge and experience in the investment field relevant to the specific type of product or service
- Financial situation
- Investment objectives

Suitability includes ensuring that:

- Any recommendations meet a customer's investment objectives
- Customers can financially bear any related investment risk consistent with their investment objectives
- Customers have the necessary experience and knowledge to understand the risks involved in the transaction

When considering the client's investment objectives, MiFID requires that firms must obtain, where relevant, information on the length of time the client wishes to hold the investment, their risk-taking preferences, risk profile and the purposes of the investment.

7. The client's financial situation

Firms must obtain, where relevant, information on the source and extent of the client's regular income, assets and regular financial commitments.

8. Streamlined advice collecting proportionate levels of information

A firm should not recommend that a client purchase an investment product unless they have a reasonable basis for believing that they can afford the new commitment. This requires the firm to consider the client's level of indebtedness and access to liquid cash to meet an emergency. The following should also be considered. Whether:

- The client wants a service that provides advice on their wider financial needs, rather than advice on a specific need
- The firm considers that the client's circumstances are too complex for the nature and scope of its service
- It is not possible to provide advice on the specific need on which the client wants advice without looking at the client's wider circumstances
- The client's debt is considered too high
- The client has insufficient emergency savings given the firm's process and product suite
- The client's desired investment horizon is too short given the asset allocation of the range of funds on offer
- The client indicates that he or she requires a service which takes existing investments into account, whereas the service on offer does not do so

- The client's appetite for risk or capacity for loss is not met through the particular products which might be offered
- The client does not have sufficient knowledge or experience for any of the products offered through the streamlined advice service

9. Relying on information

A firm is entitled to rely on the information provided by clients, unless it is aware that the information is manifestly out of date, inaccurate or incomplete. Firms should take reasonable steps to ensure that the information they do collect is reliable. Those steps include making sure that clients understand the importance of providing accurate and up-to-date information, ensuring that all tools used in the suitability assessment process are appropriate and fit for purpose, and checking for consistency of client information, including any obvious inaccuracies.

For ongoing relationships with a client, such as advice or portfolio management services, firms must have, and be able to demonstrate, effective processes for maintaining adequate and up-to-date information about their clients.

10. Existing information held by a firm

The firm should make sure they have all the information necessary to make a suitable recommendation. They should check against the client's history with their own firm if they are able to do so. If not, they should confirm with the client that all the information the client has given is complete and correct and reminding them of the importance of telling the firm about all relevant matters.

11. Considering existing investments

The firm may consider that in the particular instance information about the client's existing investments is not necessary for a suitability assessment, and therefore can proceed without it.

12. Asking clients to 'self-assess' suitability

The assessment of suitability is a core element of providing a personal recommendation. Firms must not create any ambiguity or confusion about their responsibilities in the suitability assessment process.

13. Risk profiling

This needs to include an assessment of the customer's attitude to risk and their capacity for loss. Questionnaires need to avoid questions that are not clearly worded, vague, or use double negatives or complex language that the customer may not understand. They also need to avoid questions which are not suitable for use with the firm's customer base, for example, because they assume the client has particular knowledge or experience or are structured in a way that could invite different answers. Poorly worded risk descriptions with unclear or misleading descriptions are bad practice, as is an inappropriate approach to scoring question answers and middle answers.

14. Firm responsibilities

Firms are responsible for ensuring that their personal recommendations are suitable. MiFID II will require firms to ensure that all tools, such as risk assessment profiling tools or tools to assess a client's knowledge and experience, employed in the suitability assessment process, are fit for purpose and are appropriately designed for use with their clients, with any limitations identified and actively mitigated through the suitability assessment process.

Appendix 3 – References and resources

1   http://www.deloitte.co.uk/mobileuk2015/

2   Push Doctor's 2015 Digital Health Report

3   The institutionalisation of customer service. Martin
     Wheatley, Managing Director, FCA

4   TR15/12: Wealth management firms and private banks:
     suitability of investment portfolios, FCA, 2015

5   Determinants of Portfolio Performance, Financial
     Analysts Journal, July/August 1986 Gary P. Brinson, L.
     Randolph Hood, Gilbert L. Beebower

6   Determinants of Portfolio Performance II: An Update,
     Financial Analysts Journal, May/June 1991 Gary P.
     Brinson, Brian D. Singer and Gilbert L. Beebower

7   Prospect Theory: An Analysis of Decision under Risk,

Daniel Kahneman and Amos Tversky, Econometrica, Vol. 47, No. 2., March 1979

8   http://www.nationalnumeracy.org.uk/

9   http://www.paulcraven.com/

10 Finalised guidance, assessing suitability: Establishing the risk a customer is willing and able to take and making a suitable investment selection. Financial Services Authority, March 2011

11 What makes an investor 'experienced'?, Financial Ombudsman Service, 2005 http://www.financial-ombudsman.org.uk/publications/ombudsman-news/48/investor-experienced.htm

12 Conduct of Business Sourcebook, section 10.2, FCA https://www.handbook.fca.org.uk/handbook/COBS.pdf

13 Can you trust your bank?, BBC *Panorama*, June 2011 http://www.bbc.co.uk/news/uk-13744752

14 IFA Census, NMG Consulting, 2004 onwards http://nmg-group.com/businesses/nmg-consulting/

15 Business Plan 2016/17, Financial Conduct Authority

16 The regulation of advice–recommendations post FAMR, Tracey McDermott, Acting Chief Executive, FCA, April 2016 https://www.fca.org.uk/news/speeches/regulation-advice-%E2%80%93-recommendations-post-famr

17 FCA Advice Unit. The Advice Unit is part of Project Innovate. It provides regulatory feedback to firms developing automated models that seek to deliver lower cost advice to consumers. https://www.fca.org.uk/firms/project-innovate-and-innovation-hub/advice-unit

18 Finalised Guidance, FG15/1: Clarifying the boundaries and exploring the barriers to market development, FCA, 2015

19 Financial Advice Market Review, Final report, HM Treasury, FCA, March 2016

20 Amending the definition of financial advice: consultation response. HMT, February 2017

21 Jeopardy: The IBM Challenge https://www.youtube.com/watch?v=P0Obm0DBvwI

22 Mental Accounting Matters, Richard Thaler, Journal of Behavioral Decision Making, 12, 1999. https://faculty.chicagobooth.edu/Richard.Thaler/research/pdf/MentalAccounting.pdf

23 Technology Grows Financial Advisors' Practices, reported in *Financial Advisor* magazine, 29 October, 2015

24 The Emerging Digital Advisor, Aite, Pershing, BNY Mellon, October 2015 https://www.pershing.com/_global-assets/pdf/the-emerging-digital-advisor.pdf

25 Retail Direct Firms and Digital Advice Providers 2015: Addressing Millennials, the Mass Market, and Robo Advice, Cerulli Associates, November, 2015

26 Future of Digital Financial Advice, Heidrick & Struggles with CFP Board, Centre for Financial Planning, December 2016

27 Wealth and Asset Management 2021: Preparing for Transformative Change, Roubini Thoughtlab, 2016

28 Tomorrow's Lawyers: An Introduction to Your Future, Richard Susskind, 2013

29 ABTA 2004: Web holiday sales hit record levels, 26 November 2004 www.travelmole.com

30 Travel Agents–UK, Mintel, December 2012. Also reported in *Daily Mail,* 30 June 2012

31 Bridging the advice gap: Delivering investment products in a post-RDR world, Deloitte, 2012

32 A basic advice regime for the sale of stakeholder products, CP11/04 June 2004 http://www.fsa.gov.uk/pubs/cp/cp04_11.pdf

33 http://theleanstartup.com/

34 Smarter Communications and Suitability Reports, Guidance Note, Association of Professional Advisers. December 2016

35 Thinking, Fast and Slow, Daniel Kahneman, 2011

36 Help in defined contribution plans: 2006 through 2012, Financial Engines and AON Hewitt

37 Financial inclusion. Improving the financial health of the nation, Financial Inclusion Commission, March 2015

38 How financial services lost its mojo–and how it can get it back, PWC, 2014

39 Global Trust in Financial Services, Edelman trustbarometer, 2016

40 When choice is demotivating: can one desire too much of a good thing? Sheena S. Iynegar and Mark R. Lepper, *Journal of Personality and Social Psychology*, 200 vol. 79

41 Nudge: Improving Decisions About Health, Wealth and Happiness, Cass R Sunstein and Richard H Thaler, 2009

42 Saving and Investments Customer Journey, SixthSense, YouGov 2012

43 Medium and Long-Term Retail Saving in the UK, A Review, HM Treasury, July 2002

44 *Cockpit Confidential: Everything You Need to Know About Air Travel*, Patrick Smith, 2013

45 FCA Conduct of Business Sourcebook, Chapter

9, Suitability (including basic advice) https://www.handbook.fca.org.uk/handbook/COBS/9/2.pdf

46 Vulnerability exposed: The consumer experience of vulnerability in financial services, FCA, 2014 https://www.fca.org.uk/publication/research/vulnerability-exposed-research.pdf

47 Finalised Guidance, Simplified Advice, FSA, March 2012

48 GC17/4: Financial Advice Market Review (FAMR): Implementation part 1. Guidance consultation, April 2017

49 Building a robust and efficient review process–a look at the Dynamic Planner approach, Finance & Technology Research Centre, 2015

50 https://www.yodlee.com/

51 https://www.mint.com/

52 http://www.sammedia.com/

53 https://www.moneydashboard.com/

54 https://www.gov.uk/government/news/pensions-dashboard-prototype-to-be-ready-by-spring-2017

55 https://www.bba.org.uk/news/reports/digital-disruption-uk-banking-report/#.WJdbVVOLSpo

56 https://financialengines.com/education-center/1-trillion-in-retirement-assets/

57 https://www.digitalwealthinsights.com/

58 https://www.motifinvesting.com/

59 https://www.etoro.com/

60 http://www.iii.co.uk/community/

61 https://aws.amazon.com/machine-learning/

62 https://studio.azureml.net/

63 https://www.waze.com/

64 GC17/4: Financial Advice Market Review (FAMR): Implementation part 1, April 2017.

Illustrations designed by Design City.

Praise for Catching the FinTech Wave

"A 'must read' for any CEO, CMO, CTO or other member of the C suite running an advice firm, life office, platform, or asset manager. Equally essential reading for Fintech start-ups to help them learn about the realities of the world they want to work in."

Ian McKenna, CEO of Finance & Technology Research Centre

"An excellent read. Knowledgeable, insightful, topical."

Rory Percival, consultant and formerly
Technical Specialist at FCA

"At the Personal Finance Society we believe there is a significant opportunity for the advice profession to play a key role in bridging the advice gap by utilising new technologies. Catching the FinTech Wave is a great reference for any firm seeking to benefit from new technologies in the financial advice sector."

Keith Richards, Chief Executive Officer, Personal Finance Society

"An authoritative guide from one of the industry's proven innovators"

David Dalton-Brown, Director General TISA and formerly Executive Director Fidelity Funds Network

"I have long been a believer that robust technology sits at the heart of every strong financial planning business. However many remain fearful and unsure which way to turn… this guide from one the market's key players will absolutely help you grasp the opportunities and take the leap of faith needed to transform your business model. A great in depth but equally succinct piece."

Stephen Gazard, Group Managing Director, Intrinsic. Formerly Managing Director, Sesame Bankhall Group

"A compelling read for those building Financial Services Firms, it steers thinking and actions towards the huge potential that exists for those that embrace the content"

Malcolm Streatfield, Chief Executive Lighthouse Group PLC

"Most of us agree that the only viable future for advice to the mass affluent needs at least an element of digital automation. But how to do it? You can either take a year to ponder this problem and hit the conference circuit, or take a few hours to read a book from someone who has been thinking about this for decades. Full of insights and practical tips. I found it really useful."

Holly Mackay, Founder and CEO of Boring Money

"A timely book which serves as a guide to anyone involved in financial services in understanding the implications and opportunities of digital technology on the industry"

Rob Thorpe, Head of UK Intermediary, BMO Global Asset Management

"Most organisations have the word 'digital' in their strategy, but then maybe a little light on detail? This book explains how you bring this to life in Financial Services, no matter what hat you're wearing. Insightful and relevant."

Brian Gabriel, Portfolio Director (IFA) AVIVA

"Delivering personal financial plans demands supporting technology now. Catching the FinTech Wave not only surveys a wide range of options, but actually explains in brilliant fashion how to implement! And the latter is very hard to find."

Tom Sheridan, CEO, Seven Investment Management

"This entertaining read is full of insights from a pioneer in this industry with nearly two decades of experience. With the market for automated advice set to take off spectacularly, this timely book is essential reading for anyone involved in FinTech advice or financial planning."

Professor Chris Brooks, ICMA Centre, Henley Business School, University of Reading.

"There's hard headed advice and no gushing here. Goss highlights the pitfalls of implementation and the inevitable outcome of thoughtless digitisation: the delivery of unsuitable advice at scale. A robust and overdue road map to building a 21st century practice!"

William Trout, Head of Wealth Management Research, Celent.

'Ben is an innovative and considered thinker, and a clear and engaging writer. For FinTech aficionados and Luddites alike, you'll feel better prepared if you read this book.'

Mark Brandis, Managing Partner, Libertine London